CW01203298

TINGVELLE

A HISTORY OF THINGWALL AND OTHER NORTH WIRRAL FARMING VILLAGES

by
Greg Dawson

First published 1993.

Second Edition 2005

Copyright Greg Dawson 2005

ISBN 0-9522598-4-2

Published by Dawson Publishing (of Irby).
Printed by INPRINT, King Street, Wallasey.
Typesetting by DAISYWHEEL, Bell Road, Wallasey
Re-typeset by Terence Greenwood 2005

£7.50

CONTENTS

A History of Thingwall and North Wirral.   1

How the Dawsons Came to Thingwall.   7

Thingwall Boundary.   10

A Walk around Thingwall, Summer 1993.

    Thingwall Road East to Thingwall Corner.   10

    Thingwall Corner to Sparks Lane.   15

    Lower Thingwall Lane and Basset Hound Area.   18

    Holmwood Drive and Reservoir Area.   24

    Sparks Lane.   26

    Thingwall Hill, Quarry Lane, Mill Road.   29

    Thingwall Road East to Sparks Lane.   35

    Seven Acres Lane and Heswall Mount.   38

The Last Farmer in Thingwall.   44

The Greatest Local Tragedy.   45

Life in Thingwall and North Wirral Years Ago.   46

The Irish, Welsh, Germans and "Akbar" Lads.   48

Soldiers.   49

Farming.   50

Pits.   53

Poaching.   54

Transport.   56

Walking.   57

Employment.   59

Sport.   63

Old Sayings and Amusing Characters.   64

Unusual Facts Noted.   66

Thingwall Commons and Woodland.   66

The Three Brooks of Thingwall.   67

Field Names.   68

Lane and Road Names.   70

The Farming Community of Landican.   71

The Three Farms.   72

Tied Cottages.   73

Woodchurch.   76

Charities.   77

The Robin Family.   78

Home Farm, Woodchurch.   78

Some Woodchurch Families of the 1920s.   80

Wirral Castles.   84

Local Wildlife.   85

A Well Known Local Countryman   86

Some 18th Century North Wirral Names Still Surviving.   87

Some Local Pubs of Yesteryear.   87

Parish Registers, Wills and Maps.   88 to 96

ILLUSTRATIONS

Cover Photo   PEAR TREE COTTAGE
The young lady pictured is Violet Croker

Page 9   HOLM COTTAGE

11   TOP HOUSE FARM

13   POPLAR COTTAGE

14   THINGWALL HALL

17   T MODEL FORD

21   LOWER THINGWALL LANE

22   BARN FARM

32   MILL STONES

34   THINGWALL WINDMILL

42   BENTY HEATH FARM

43   THINGWALL HOUSE

43   WOODFINLOW COTTAGE

43   MOLLY BOWDEN

44   GEORGE BOWDEN

50   THE WILBRAHAM BROTHERS

52   MORETON CROSS

58   NESTON COLLIERY

60   IRBY VILLAGE

66   WOODSIDE FERRY

72   HOMEFARM, LANDICAN

74   LANDICAN LANE

75   LANDICAN LANE (FARM VIEW)

76   THE POPLARS LANDICAN LANE

79   ARROWE PARK GATES

82   CHURCH TERRACE, WOODCHURCH

83   HORSE AND JOCKEY

83   LEE'S SMITHY

86   ALF OXTON

Back cover   THINGWALL CORNER (To-day)

DEDICATION

This book is a tribute to my Mother and Father, Peter and Hilda Dawson, George and Molly Bowden and all other local senior citizens of their era.

People with whom I spent so many happy childhood hours and who gave me so much guidance in my youth. Tenant farmers, tradesmen and labourers of Wirral who struggled through life's hardships and tragedies. Men who made the best living they could for themselves and their families through sheer hard work, with no state benefits.

Widows who took in washing and made ends meet as best they could, but still managed to bring up a respectable family.

Husbands and wives who stuck together when richer or poorer, in sickness and in health. (There was more than enough of sickness and plenty of being poorer.)

They had little or nothing compared to us today, but that never dampened their sense of humour. They took life on the chin and when there were serious problems, these people faced up to them and saw them through.

ACKNOWLEDGMENTS.

Thanks must go to all the local people who have helped and encouraged me to write this book. Also to Cheshire County Council Archives and Local Studies and Birkenhead Reference Library for access to their records and for the help and patience of their staff.

Special thanks must go to three local historians, Derek Young, Ian Boumphrey and Jim O'Neil. To Derek and Ian for their suggestions and providing me with most of the photographs in this book and to Jim for patiently reading my 'dummy runs' and giving me so much guidance.

Thanks also to the Vicar and P.C.C. of Bidston, and to the Rector and P.C.C. of Woodchurch, for their kind permission to quote from the parish registers in the care of Cheshire County Council.

Two other people eventually got me 'off the ground'. Fred Howard of Pensby and my Sister Mrs. Geraldine Ryan of Thingwall.

Fred patiently spent many hours giving me computer tuition and saved my bacon many times when I made so many silly mistakes.

Our Geraldine was my 'legs'. She pursued and solved many queries for me while I was tied up with work and herself found out a tremendous amount about our family.

A HISTORY OF THINGWALL AND NORTH WIRRAL

In Roman times Wirral was inhabited by Celtic Britons.

The Romans controlled Wirral for about 350 years but few Romans settled here. Their Chester based legions patrolled the peninsula and they had a look-out station and outpost at Meols.

There have been a number of finds from Roman occupation. In 1834, workmen quarrying in Oxton on a hill called *The Arno* found a small hoard of Roman coins. On this hill could have been a small camp.

In 1850 when Wallasey Pool, then a natural tidal creek, was being converted into Birkenhead docks, workmen discovered a solid oak bridge 100 feet long resting on rock at each end. Traces of a Roman house were recently unearthed in a garden in Irby and many Roman artifacts and coins have been found in Meols and a few around Thurstaston.

In the 1st century A.D., Wirral was part of the territory of the Cornavii Tribe, but by the 4th century they had been displaced by another Celtic tribe – The Deceangli. This powerful tribe inhabited an area from the Lleyn peninsula across North Wales to Cheshire including Wirral.

The Romans left about 410 A.D. and eventually Wirral came under the rule of the Celtic kingdom of Gwynedd.

Celtic Christians began coming to Wirral in the 5th century and eventually dedicated three North Wirral churches to Celtic saints, in Landican, Wallasey and West Kirby.

Woodchurch, originally part of Landican, was dedicated to St. Tegan 'the traveller'. *Llan* is Welsh for church and *Tegan* was a Welsh saint. *Llan Tegan*, the church of Tegan became Landican.

Another Celtic saint who may have given his name to Landican was Tecwyn, the Breton who became patron saint of Llandecwyn, near Harlech. However this is thought less likely.

St. Bridget's Church in West Kirby is dedicated to the Irish saint, Bridget of Kildare.

St. Hilary's in Wallasey is one of only eight churches of that name in Britain. All are in Celtic areas except two. Five are in Wales, one is in Llanilar in Cornwall and the other two are in Lincoln and Wallasey.

Another Celtic place name is Dove Point at Meols, from dubh meaning black. Meols foreshore was, until comparatively recently, covered in black peat from the sunken forest. The name Dublin in Ireland means dark pool.

About this time Angles, Saxons and Jutes from northern Germany, Fresia and Jutland began to ravage the south and eastern shores of England. As they gradually conquered England the Celts submitted or fled to Cornwall, Wales or the North West.

Aethelfrith, the Anglian King of Bernicia in Northumberland, was determined to smash the powerful Welsh kingdom of Gwynedd. In 615 he defeated the Celts, captured Chester, their capital, and massacred 2,000 monks at Bangor on Dee. The Anglo Saxons drove the Welsh before them up the Wirral peninsula. Those who would not surrender fled to Wallasey to make a last stand.

In those days, Wallasey was more or less an island with the Irish Sea, River Mersey and Wallasey Pool on three sides and Leasowe, Moreton and Bidston marshes on the fourth side. When the tide was in, it covered most of the marshes making Wallasey an island stronghold. When the Anglo Saxons reached these treacherous marshes they did not attempt to cross.

The Celts were called *Wealas* which is Anglo Saxon meaning strangers. *Wealas* came to mean Welsh. *Wealas Isle* or *Welshmans Isle* has, over the years, become Wallasey.

In the same way, the Welsh Island conquered by the Anglo Saxons became known as *Angles Isle*, now Anglesey.

Apart from Wallasey, Wirral, including Thingwall, came firmly under Anglo Saxon rule and they began to settle all over the peninsula.

They called the peninsula *Wirheal*; *heal* being Saxon for corner and *Wir* a myrtle plant. The myrtle plant grew all over the boggy areas of Wirral.

Village names ending in ham or ton are Anglo Saxon meaning settlement or enclosed farmstead. For instance Eastham means manor or settlement in the east. Oxton means farmstead of the oxen and Moreton means farmstead on the marsh or mere. In documents I have seen written in the 1600s, Gayton is called Goaton, which could mean farmstead where the goats are kept.

Wirral became part of the Kingdom of Mercia, probably named after it's main border, the River Mersey, but it was the Vikings, or Norsemen as they were often called, who founded Thingwall.

The name Viking comes from the Norse word *vikingr*, a sea rover or pirate who comes from the *viks* or inlets.

In the 9th century, Norsemen, mainly from Dublin and the Isle of Man, raided Wirral and the West. By the year 901 there were 12 Viking settlements in Wirral. Dublin was a fortified stronghold for trading and raiding, for plunder and slaves, but in 902 it was over run by the Irish King Caerbhall of Leinster. Many Vikings then fled Ireland.

One band, under the leadership of Hingamund, took to their boats and sailed east. After being driven from Anglesey they sailed up the River Dee and attacked Chester.

Eventually, the Saxon Princess Ethelflaed of Mercia, King Alfred the Great's daughter, granted Hingamund land in Wirral. Over the next 50 years, Norsemen, mainly from Ireland and Norway, flocked to Wirral and the North West to settle. They colonized an area from Wirral to Galloway in Scotland. They were efficient farmers and it was the Norsemen who brought the plough to Britain.

They settled mainly on the more fertile western side of the peninsula as many of the village names tell us.

Thingwall means 'assembly place', *Thing* being Norse for Parliament and '*Wall*' from the Norse word *Vellir*, a field.

The Vikings assembled in Thingwall yearly or twice yearly to hold their parliament at Cross Hill to discuss, review and administer their laws.

They held the same meetings in the Thingwall area of Wavertree in Liverpool, at Tynwald in the Isle of Man, Dingwall in Scotland, the Althing in Iceland and Logthing in the Faroe Islands. It is recorded that in the year 910 forty Viking ships anchored in Wallasey Pool for the meeting of the Thingwall parliament.

The names of Viking settlements often end in 'by' which is Scandinavian, meaning farmstead or settlement. Irby means farmstead of the Irish, Pensby means farmstead on the hill and West Kirby means West Church Village. In Scotland churches are still called Kirks. From this village or *by* we get the local *by-law*. Anyone outside these laws became an *out-law*.

The people of Wirral, like the village names, became a mixture of Welsh, Saxon and Viking.

In 1066 the Normans invaded England. The forefathers of these invaders were Norsemen, or Northmen, who, in 911 settled in that French peninsula which became known as Northmandy and eventually, Normandy.

After the Battle of Hastings, the rest of England was gradually brought under Norman control. In 1070 William the Conqueror subdued Cheshire. As a punishment for resisting William, many Cheshire manors were laid waste. In Wirral, Landican, Storeton, Neston, Little Meols, Noctorum, Willaston and Poulton-cum-Spital were destroyed.

England was divided between William the Conqueror's Earls and Barons.

There were 51 manors in Wirral. The Bishop of Chester held one, the Abbey of St. Werburgh held eight and the Earl of Chester held 42.

About 2,000 people lived in Wirral, a quarter of Cheshire's population. In those days, Cheshire included part of what later became the Welsh county of Flintshire.

Hugh Lupus (The Wolf), William's nephew, was the first Earl of Chester and he was responsible for keeping the marauding Welsh at bay.

From his Cheshire lands, Hugh raised about £200 a year and his estates in other shires raised about £700. This income financed his Welsh campaigns.

Hugh gave many manors in North Wales and Cheshire to Robert de Rodelant (Baron of Rhuddlan), who was his cousin and Commander in Chief. These included *Eswelle* (Heswall) and *Turstaletone* (Thurstaston). William FitzNigel was granted *Bernstone* (Barnston) and many more manors.

William Malbank, Baron of Nantwich, Hugh's most powerful tenant, was granted Thingwall, Landican and about 40 other Cheshire manors.

These barons could not control such large areas without the help of 'under tenants' to look after individual estates. Durand was entrusted with Thingwall.

In the Domesday Book, Thingwall is spelt Tuigvelle. This may be a transcription error for Tingvelle. It must have been very difficult for the French speaking Normans to understand all the different dialects and put names to all the villages.

Landican is spelt *Landechene* in the Domesday Book. This could be because in those days, Woodchurch church was probably built of timber and French for oak is *dechene*.

The Domesday Book records that the Norman baron William Malbank held Thingwall and Durand held it from him. The Saxon, Winterlet, held it previously and he was a free man. There was one hide paying tax and land for two ploughs. In lordship one [plough] and there were two slaves, one villager and one smallholder with another plough. Valued at 8 shillings (40p) before 1066, Thingwall was only valued at 5 shillings (25p) in 1086 when the Domesday Book was written.

Landican was also held by William Malbank, previously it was held by the Saxon, Aescwulf, who was a free man. There were seven hides paying tax and land for eight ploughs. In lordship one [plough] and there was a priest, nine villagers, seven smallholders and four Frenchmen with five ploughs between them. Landican was valued at 50 shillings (£2-50) before 1066, after being laid waste in 1070, it had not recovered to its previous value and was only worth 40 shillings (£2-00) in 1086. The priest would be from the Wooden Church from which Woodchurch derived its name.

Landican was the second most important manor in Wirral, both in value and population. Only Eastham was bigger and more valuable.

A *hide* was about 120 acres and was used for tax assessment. It was not measured or paced out but an estimated amount of land a man needed to feed his family for a year. Therefore, a hide in an area with poor land would be bigger than a hide in an area with rich soil.

A plough was a ploughing team of eight oxen. In lordship one, meant that the under tenant had one plough and farmed land himself.

Landless villagers were called *slaves*. Smallholders were middle class peasants with a small amount of land and a *villager* was a higher class of peasant with the most land. *Frenchmen* were immigrants from France since 1066.

Some villages such as Upton and Caldy had an acre or two of meadow. This was common land for hay.

Radmen or riding men were recorded in some villages such as Upton, Eastham and Meols. They had to perform duties such as delivering messages, escorting their lords and keeping an eye on local roads and bridges, making sure they were kept up to scratch. Riding men or *Rad knights* were only found in counties such as Cheshire, which bordered the Welsh marches.

In areas where the majority of people were of Viking origin, such as Lancashire, land was measured in *carucates* and *bovates*. These were the Scandinavian equivalents of the English *hides* and *virgates*.

About 80 per cent of land in cultivation in 1914 was already under the plough in 1086. The population of England was about two million in Norman times.

William the Conqueror was very strict on law and order. Fines and punishments of all sorts are recorded in the Domesday Book, for all kinds of offences.

For instance in one border region, if a Welshman stole a woman or a cow and was caught, he had to restore what he had stolen and forfeit 20 shillings (£1-00). A law recorded in Chester stated that if a widow had unlawful intercourse she was fined 20 shillings (£1-00) but a girl would only be fined 10 shillings (50p).

Robert de Rodelant was killed by the Welsh on the 3rd of July, 1088. He was out with only one soldier when they were surprised by a Welsh force at Deganwy. He drew his sword and stood his ground but as he was a renowned warrior no Welshman would face him. Archers were brought up and Robert died in a hail of arrows.

His lands passed on to others. His Wallasey lands, for instance, passed to the Baron of Halton, who held land in other parts of Wirral including Greasby.

In Norman times and the Middle Ages, the upper classes fought as an occupation for honour and booty. Many like Robert were killed and estates changed hands.

Powerful families such as the Stanleys, Masseys, Domvilles, Whitmores, Troutbecks, Pooles and many more came to possess estates all over Wirral and elsewhere.

Wirral was a lawless area, covered in forest, heath and marsh. The so-called gentry were, in many cases, little more than gangsters. They roamed Wirral and further afield, murdered, robbed and poached.

In the 1330's, John Domville was in possession of Thingwall, Oxton, Barnston, Brimstage and other manors. The Domvilles were often in trouble, leading poaching gangs with packs of dogs on raids in Wirral and Lancashire.

The Domville estates passed to the Hulse family, then the Troutbecks and eventually to the Earl of Shrewsbury.

The Stanleys, a very powerful family, held Hooton, Storeton, Rhuddlan Castle and many more estates including the Isle of Man in later years.

Cheshire archers were second to none. Companies of Wirral archers forded the River Dee from *Shotwick Castle* in the Welsh wars of the 13th century and in the 14th century, sailed from Burton Point to Ireland. Under the command of families such as Stanley, Massey and Poole, these archers were a vital part of the English army.

Richard II had a personal bodyguard of Cheshire men recruited by Sir John Stanley of Hooton. Some of these men would have come from North Wirral and the Stanley estates at Hooton and Storeton, and probably some from Woodchurch Parish, which included Thingwall and Landican.

In Cromwellian times, Wirral was Royalist. John Stanley was a staunch Royalist and was executed by Cromwell in 1651. Cromwell died in 1658. Eventually, Charles II was restored to the throne and Royalist lands were restored to their original owners.

In the 1660's Thingwall was claimed by the Earl of Shrewsbury and Sir William Stanley. The Stanley lands passed to Sir Robert Vyner, the London goldsmith and banker. In the last century, about one third of Thingwall's 371 acres belonged to Lord Vyner.

According to documents relating to the hearth tax, it appears there were only six houses in Thingwall in 1664 and they were occupied by the following families, Dellamore, Hanckock, Watt, Birons, Lowe and Flecher.

In 1792 there were seven farms and a mill in Thingwall. The farms were owned by John Banks Jnr., Thomas Ashbrook, John Wade, Henry Whittle, John Bellis, Robert Capper and Robert Vyner esq. The Whittles and the Cappers were owner occupiers, but the other landowners rented their properties to tennants. The tenant farmers were Joseph Meacock, Brian Watmough, Thomas Davies and Daniel Broster who rented two farms.

The village community would have been pretty well self- sufficient. There was a flour mill and farmers killed and butchered their own animals, grew their own fruit and vegetables and even brewed their own ale, called *swig*.

Thingwall's 371 acres make it a small township compared to it's neighbours; Storeton 1,380, Barnston 1,068, Irby 900, Arrowe 752, Landican 605 and Wirral's largest township, Willaston, with 1,994 acres.

The only smaller township bordering Thingwall, is Pensby, with 335 acres all belonging to John Baskerville Glegg in the mid 1800's.

In 1801 there were 14,550 people living in the boundary of the old City of Chester, but the entire population of Wirral was only 10,744.

Thingwall's population was 52, Pensby 31, Landican 45, Arrowe 96, Irby 105, Birkenhead 110, Barnston 129, Oxton 137, Storeton 180, Heswall cum Oldfield 323, Tranmere, the second largest Wirral town 353 and Neston, by far the most populous town, had 1,486 inhabitants.

By the 1840's Thingwall's population had risen to 76 living in 12 farms and smallholdings and four houses. Thingwall Hamlet was situated down what is today Lower Thingwall Lane and there were five farms.

This area has probably been the site of Thingwall since ancient times. It is a sheltered, well-watered spot with a brook and four ancient wells, now covered. Also, ancient footpaths and roads radiated out in all directions to Landican, Storeton, Barnston, Woodchurch, Pensby, Irby and Greasby.

In the last century, Thingwall was spelt *Thingwell*, probably how it was pronounced. This can be seen on old gravestones in Woodchurch graveyard.

In 1850 most of the land was owned by five people: Robert Vyner, 114 acres, Joseph Roberts 88; John Leech 56; Elizabeth Wade 30 and John Shaw 25.

There were several minor land owners, among them the Cappers who ran the *Windmill Yard* and rented a smallholding. They were quite an important family, milling in Thingwall for about 160 years.

Obviously the village men were mainly engaged in farming, milling and some quarrying. In the 1850's there was also a shoe-maker, watch-maker, coachman, tailor, smith, servants, gardeners at *Arrowe* and *Thingwall Halls* and a gentleman merchant. In the 1860's there was also an inn-keeper and in the 1870's a white smith. White smiths worked in tin and polished metals.

In 1851 Thingwalls population had increased to 96 living in 17 dwellings and in 1881 there were 162 people and 30 houses. More houses sprang up on Thingwall Hill, known as Mill Brow in those days, and a few more were scattered about the rest of the township.

By the turn of the century Thingwall was really starting to mushroom.

It was now a village of three parts like Pensby. Higher Thingwall up Mill Road on Thingwall Hill, Lower Thingwall down Lower Thingwall Lane and Heathfields.

Heathfields was an area roughly from what is now Ambleside Close to the top of Seven Acres Lane. This is reflected in ten field names and three old house names with the word Heath in them.

In 1911 the census records 200 residents in Thingwall and a large increase to 652 by 1931.

The latter figure was greatly increased by the staff and patients of the Childrens Hospital at Thingwall corner and the Childrens Sanatorium down Holmwood Drive where the B.U.P.A. hospital now stands.

Pensby in those days was 'Higher' up round Kylemore Drive area, 'Lower' round *The Pensby Hotel* area and 'Newtown' built in the 1880s between Gills Lane and Fender Way. Actually, Newtown is in the township of Barnston but it has always been classed as Pensby.

HOW THE DAWSONS CAME TO THINGWALL

The name Dawson, spelt Daweson, is mentioned in documents from the Middle Ages and means son of David. Dawe being old English for David. Names ending in 'son' are more numerous in the North of England and Scotland than in the South and many have a Scandinavian background.

Dawson is a fairly common name in Scotland, being a branch of the Clan Davidson, from north of Inverness. There are also a fair number in Ireland.

Many of the old records are faded and badly written. Dawson is sometimes spelt, Doson, in the 1600's and Irby is spelt, Eirby, Erby and Erbie.

There were Dawson's farming in Irby before 1605 and we are one of the oldest farming families in North Wirral.

Peter Dawson, born in Irby in 1614 had five children, one of them, also called Peter, was my direct ancestor. In 1672 he married Jane Lakes of Great Neston by special licence, as our family did in the 1600s and 1700s and not by banns. They had four sons and a daughter.

Their eldest son Nathaniel was born in 1678 and grew up to be an Irby Yeoman. Nathaniel's wife Esther, (nee Webster, who came from a wealthy Bidston farming family), had three sons and five daughters. In the 1740's they retired to a small farm in Tranmere, which was two villages in those days, Holt Hill and Hinderton. Nathaniel died there in 1753 aged 75 and his lands, property and money was shared amongst his family.

His eldest son, John, inherited his Irby estate and also became a Yeoman of Moreton, his second son, William (who died a bachelor) became a Yeoman of Saughall Massie and his third son, Thomas was a Little Meols Husbandman. (Yeomen owned their farms and Husbandmen were tenants farmers.)

Like his parents before him, John and his wife Elizabeth,(nee Maddock, daughter of a Moreton Yeoman,) had a large family, four boys and three girls. His three surviving sons were John, Nathaniel and Peter, who died a bachelor. In 1763 John bought a considerable amount of land from the Rev. John Crookhall, Rector of Woodchurch, for £1,400 and he leased a large amount of land from Lord Robert Vyner and Sir Philip Egerton of Leasowe Castle.

He had four farms in Moreton and one in Irby and lived at *Watts House Farm*, Woodchurch. In 1779 John died, leaving sons, John and Peter his Moreton and Upton property and Nathaniel his Irby estate.

In 1775, on their farm in Moreton, Nathaniel's wife Catherine, (nee Young of Capenhurst), gave birth to their first child, William, my Great, Great, Great Grandfather.

Catherine died aged only 28 and Nathaniel eventually married Mary Stanley of Storeton, who gave him five daughters.

One of them, Ellen, married Henry Brown, a Gentleman farmer from Grange and had a son, Charles Dawson Brown who became the cotton broker and scholar, who founded Wirral's first museum.

Even today, there is a Charles Dawson Brown prize at Calday Grange Grammar School.

William married Mary Ann Bradley, (sometimes spelt Marrianne), who was born in Holyhead in 1778 and they lived on the family's farm in Irby Village.

In those days it was called Dawsons Farm and is now known as *Yew Tree Farm*.

William owned land along what is now Thingwall Road, from the village to Harrock Wood, some up Limbo Lane and a field on the Pensby side of Harrock Wood.

Mary Ann had three sons at the farm, James Bradley in 1798, John in 1800 and Peter in 1802.

In 1803, William became a flour dealer and moved to Primrose Hill, Liverpool with his wife and family.

At this time the family owned six farms, were tenants of three and leased land and property in Moreton, Upton, Irby, Storeton and Liverpool. This is to be seen in land deeds, eight wills and scores of land tax documents stored in the archives of Cheshire Records Office. Most of the farms were left to female members of the family and were lost to the Dawson name.

In Liverpool, Mary Ann had two more children, a daughter, Mary Ann Washington, and a son, Nathaniel. Nathaniel became a landowner in the village of Hoose, now part of Hoylake and his granddaughter, Marianne Bradley Dawson (born in Thompson Street, Tranmere in 1866) was awarded the M.B.E. in 1939 for nursing. She died in 1961 aged 95.

After a few years William became a cotton broker, whilst tenant Richard Oxton rented his farm. In 1812, William sold the Irby farm, which had been in the family since the 1600s.

His second son John, my Great Great Grandfather married Frankby farmer's daughter, Martha Broster at Woodchurch Church in 1825. John worked in Liverpool as a wheelwright and in 1828 he moved to Chester Street, Birkenhead and worked at Lairds Shipyard as a ships joiner. In 1835 he eventually became tenant of a small 10½ acre farm in Holm Lane, Oxton, owned by the Earl of Shrewsbury.

The old white farm cottage is still standing. Entering Holm Lane from Woodchurch Road, it is the second house on the right, just past *the Swan Hotel*. In those days it was number six, now it is number eight.

Martha had five children and John worked as a master joiner and wheelwright, supplementing his income with their small farm. Their eldest son, James, born in 1828, was my Great Grandfather.

James married Mary Upton, from a Spital farming family, and they lived in an old cottage in Holm Lane. Just like other cottagers in those days they kept a few pigs and poultry etc., and James worked as a house joiner. In later years he worked as a ships joiner at Lairds.

In 1859, Mary gave birth to my Grandfather, Jack, the eldest of her five children. Jack grew up to be a domestic gardener. He met and married Melina Gregory, who worked as a house maid at the Noctorum Mansion of Beausire's, the wealthy Liverpool cotton merchants.

My Grandparents started married life in 1889 at 22 Holm Lane, which was pulled down about 1907. My Grandmother's wedding present from Beausire's, was a cow, on the proviso that she supplied the mansion with milk.

From this one cow my Grandparents started their own small farm. They became tenants of a smallholding from the 1890's until 1922. Grandfather carried on doing jobbing gardening to make ends meet.

The smallholding, called *Holm Dell*, was built in about 1850. It was re-named *Holm Cottage* and is still standing up the unmade branch of Holm Lane, behind *the Swan Hotel*.

Peter Dawson, my Father, was born there in 1906, the second youngest of thirteen children, five dying in infancy.

Holm Cottage had a couple of out buildings, a well in the yard, two 2½ acre fields and one 2 acre field where Swan Motors stand and previously Swan Hill Dairy.

Grandfather had nine cows, two horses, some pigs, poultry and ran an egg and milk round locally.

The smallholding, which was owned by the Earl of Shrewsbury, was too small for such a large family. So, in 1922, they moved to *The Piggery* in Gallopers Lane, Thingwall, which my Grandfather rented from Mrs. Coxon the wife of Robert Coxon, a livestock dealer from Saughall Massie.

From Dad's tales of his youth in Thingwall in the 1920's, it is obvious he had a great affection for the village, it's people and it's way of life. During my own childhood in the 1950's and 60's, I too developed a great interest in Thingwall and it's surrounding villages.

Grandad Dawson with one of his terriers, outside the smallholding, *Holm Cottage*, today a private house. The man behind him is believed to be odd job man George Curtis.

THINGWALL BOUNDARY

The township of Thingwall, totalling 371 acres, is bordered by Pensby, Irby, Arrowe, Landican, Storeton, and Barnston is five miles from Birkenhead and five miles from Neston.

The boundary runs down the centre of Pensby Road from opposite *the Pensby Hotel* to the bend by the top of Whaley Lane. It then carries on in a straight line between Heathfield flats and Shakeshafts old cottage *Three Ways*, aptly named.

Then the boundary follows what was the ancient drainage ditch and hawthorn hedge separating, on the Irby side, Anderson Close and Thingwall Drive from Ambleside Close and Heywood Boulevard on the Thingwall side.

On reaching Thingwall Road East, it follows the road to Thingwall Corner. Then the hawthorn footpath hedge starting at the stile opposite the roundabout. This hedge runs toward Landican and after a short distance, Landican Brook appears from a land drain.

The ancient hawthorn hedge and Landican Brook are the Landican/Thingwall boundary. One field before Storeton railway line, Landican Brook joins Prenton Brook where two dales meet. Here Thingwall ends. Prenton Brook, running from the direction of Barnston, becomes the Storeton-Thingwall boundary until reaching the foot bridge on Barnston Dale public footpath.

Here the small tributary called Dale End Brook, running down from Holmwood Drive and Dale End, becomes the Barnston-Thingwall boundary. At Dale End on the junction of Barnston Road and Holmwood Drive, the little brook flows under Barnston Road. It is little more than a ditch on the other side of the road. The ditch and the hawthorn hedge run down between *Wacko's Pits*, borders Gwendoline Close, separates Rylands Park, Thingwall from Dale View Close, Barnston and passes alongside the Bethel Chapel on Heswall Mount to the centre of Pensby Road.
As with most ancient boundaries, Thingwall's are mainly natural water courses which generally do not alter.

A WALK AROUND THINGWALL, SUMMER 1993
Along Thingwall Road East, (formerly Irby Road),
From Thingwall Drive to Thingwall Corner.

Some Thingwall fields were worked by farms in neighbouring villages. Two such farms were *Greystones* and *Top House Farm*, both are standing on Thingwall Road close to Thingwall Drive and are today private houses.

Greystones, built about 1860, and originally called *Strawberry Cottage* is an old whitewashed sandstone cottage hidden by trees, next to Dane Court flats, just outside the Thingwall boundary, in Irby.

Jack Hammond, who worked this farm from the turn of the century and through the 1920s and 30s was the last farmer at *Greystones*. His Father and Uncles came to Wirral from Macclesfield in the 1840s to work as gardeners and gamekeepers at the *Arrowe Hall* Estate, now Arrowe Park.

Jack was born in 1860 in a lodge, which once stood at the footpath entrance to Arrowe Park opposite Thingwall Drive.

Between the wars he farmed the Thingwall fields where Heywood Boulevard is built and land in Irby were Dane Court flats are, much of which were huge clay pits. Jack grew potatoes, kept a few cows and ran a milk round.

Greystones was owned by Yates' Brewery in the 1970s. They tried to build a pub there but permission was refused.

Top House Farm, backing onto Arrowe Park golf course is at present being renovated. This farm is in fact, in Arrowe Township but it has always had strong links with Thingwall. *Arrowe* is Irish Norse meaning *little cottage*.

A shoemaker's widow, Mrs. Mary Kendrick, was born Mary Wilson in Thingwall in 1804. For several decades in the last century, Mary was tenant at *Top House Farm*, which she rented along with the land between what is today Arrowe Park and Limbo Lane from John Shaw of *Arrowe Hall*. She also rented land across the road in Thingwall and at Thingwall Corner, owned by Sir Robert Vyner.

Top House Farm. (Under renovation at the time)

Mary ran the farm with her sons John, George and daughter Ann.

Ann Kendrick became Mrs. Wainwright and took the tenancy of *Top House* over in the 1870s when her mother died.

The Kendricks still live in the area. Mary's Great Grandson, Derek Young, is a local historian.

In the 1880's, Mr. MacFarlane and his wife Jessie, both born in Scotland in 1826, took over *Top House Farm*. When they first came to Wirral, they lived in Bebington, Seacombe, then Arrowe.

The MacFarlane's had seven children. They still ran *Top House* in the 1920's when my Dad remembers Mr. MacFarlane, the tenant, being run over by a car, when riding his push-bike to church.

Ralph Leech of *Home Farm* in Landican then took over *Top House* as it stood, lock, stock and barrel. Ralph put his brother-in-law, Bill Adams, in the farm to run it for him before Bill got his own place at *Arrowe House Farm* on Bunkers Hill, now under Champion Spark Plugs.

Ron Bradbury was the next and last farmer at *Top House*. Ronny also had a butcher's stall in Birkenhead market and butcher's shop in Rock Ferry. Ron's Dad ran the farm while he concentrated on his butchery business. Ronny was a hard worker and in those days, he used to pull his fresh meat from Woodside Lairage in a hand-cart. When old Mr. Bradbury retired to a house opposite Thingwall Surgery, Ron moved from Slatey Road into the farm.

When Jack Hammond retired, *Greystones* went up for sale and Ronny Bradbury had his eye on it. At the Barnston Womens Institute, Ron's mother-in-law told a couple of women he was going to offer £500 for *Greystones*. A Scottish woman present who lived in *Rock Cottage* Sparks Lane, Thingwall, overheard her and stepped in with an offer and bought the place.

For years Ronny was kicking himself at missing out. Eventually his mother-in-law confessed to letting the cat out of the bag. Ronny took a deep breath and went out with the dog for a long walk.

Ronny and his wife, who was one of the Pyke's jewellers family, were tenants at *Top House Farm* until the 1960's when he died.

Mr. J. Alexander Duncan of Landican took over the land, which since 1917 has been owned by Lord Leverhulme' and in the 1970s his wife ran a farm shop in the out buildings, with Mrs. Bradbury.

Opposite *Top House Farm* once stood a smallholding owned by Lord Vyner called *Poplar Cottage*, built in the early 1800s and known locally as *The Thatch* because of its roof. During the middle decades of the last century it was rented by Thomas Joinson along with an acre croft and a garden. Thomas was born in Thingwall in 1767 and his wife was also born in Thingwall, in 1759. Their son, John, was an assistant gardener. Mrs. Joinson lived well into her late 90's and when she died, son John took the tenancy over.

Through the 1890's and until the 1950s the Brown family lived in *The Thatch*. John Brown, who was born in Birkenhead in 1841, lived in Wales in the 1880s before moving to Thingwall to work as a roadman. From the Great War era, Bill 'Foxy' Brown, farmed land where Thingwall Primary School and Richmond Way now stand, and also on Cross Hill opposite the reservoir, all owned by Robert Vyner.

After the Great War, Joe one of Foxy's sons bought two army horses with the old army brand on their backsides. These horses enabled the Brown's to take on contract work. 'Foxy' did a lot of work at Prenton Water Works, when a new well was sunk near Water Park Road for the Wirral Water Company.

The Thatch was demolished and some of the houses of Heywood Boulevard were built on the site in about 1960. Some of the Brown family stayed local and others moved over to Liverpool to work for the Council in the Parks and Gardens Department.

In the middle of the field Heywood Boulevard is built on, were huge clay pits, hundreds of years old and covering over an acre. The West Cheshire Water Board used to contract Roe-Bucks of Heswall in the 1920's and 30's to transport the clay for them from these pits. The clay was used to mould collars in water pipes into which was poured molten lead. The pipes were then fitted together and caulked water-tight.

The old locals reckoned *Top House Farm* and farm buildings in Landican and at *Irby Farm*, in Irby village were built from hand made bricks made with clay from these pits.

The Warrens, built in 1750 and standing opposite the junction of Thingwall Road East and Pensby Road at 199 feet above sea level, was a smallholding and is now a private house. The old-timers reckon it got its name because it was overrun with rabbits.

Poplar Cottage
This once stood opposite *Top House Farm* and was the home of a smallholder and carter, Foxy Brown.

Being on the wrong side of the road, *The Warrens* is in Arrowe. From the 1880s until after the Great War Mr. Smith and son Bill from Woodchurch were tenants. Then Bill Jordan, who became a boss on the Wirral Water Company, lived there for a very short time. After Bill moved out in about 1920, farm workers Tom, Harry and Joe Oxton from Storeton became the new tenants. Tom worked on a farm in Storeton, but his two brothers bought two one-horse carts and did council work as well as run the smallholding. In 1927, Birkenhead Corporation bought *The Warrens* and the Oxton brothers left in 1928. Joe's son Alf, lives in Pensby Road, Thingwall and Alf's son Paul and his wife Ann, live in Beaumaris Drive.

From 1929 *The Warrens* was the home of Mr. Smith the Arrowe Park forester then Scottish Woodsman, Mr Munro and his family, until 1953 when the Scott family moved in.

The land which once belonged to *The Warrens* is today a council nursery and *The Warrens* farmhouse is now the privately owned home of British kick boxing champion Garry Sandland and family.

Before Landican Road was built, from opposite Thingwall Corner to Landican Village, the quickest route to Landican was by public footpath from the stile at Thingwall Corner. For the first two fields, the path follows the old hawthorn hedge, past two massive old sandstone gate stoops and then over the footbridge and stile. From here, the right of way is through the centre of a pasture field and eventually down *the slutch hole* past *Old Hall Farm* into Landican Lane.

These first fields are known as *The Marl Fields*. They once belonged to Lord Vyner, then Robert Holdsworth, and now they are George Bowden's.

The Thingwall Corner Council Estate was built in the 1960's after *Thingwall Hall* was demolished. I remember *Thingwall Hall*. It was a massive and very impressive building. The hall was built in 1849 by Captain Lilley on two fields called *Mill Hay* and *Priests Park*.

There was a lodge, gardeners cottages, a coachhouse, stables for eight horses, a loose box, shippen, piggery, poultry yard, greenhouses and 21 acres.

Captain John Lilley was a merchant in the African Trade, as was his son-in-law who also lived at the *Hall*. He was born in Gosport and his son-in-law in Warwickshire.

Also listed at *Thingwall Hall* in 1851 were Captain Lilley's 28 year old second wife, Sarah, who was 22 years his junior and born in Cheshire, and his 1½ year old son, John. His daughters were Hannah, aged 20, born in Liverpool and 23 year old Fanny, born in Gibraltar. Captain Lilley employed 22 year old French butler, Robert Duval, 33 year old Cumberland born cook, Ann Mellor, 28 year old Cornish housemaid, Hannah Bennet, 30 year old Chester born nurse, Hannah Gill, Emma Walker aged 18 also born in Chester, and farm servant Charles Hebril, aged 16 and born in Rock Ferry.

Thingwall Hall, a country mansion built in 1849

At the hall yard lived Captain Lilley's coachman, Richard Clay and his family. Richard, aged 33 and his 31 year old wife, Elizabeth were born in Shropshire. They had a three year old son, Henry, and an eight month old daughter, Elizabeth, born in Thingwall.

Captain Lilley had a cow to provide milk and butter and a few pigs and hens at the yard which Charles Hebril looked after.

John Lilley sold *Thingwall Hall* in the 1850's, to Mr. Alexander Lafone from Liverpool, who was a merchant in the River Plate trade. He in turn sold the Hall in the 1860s to Mr. Porter, a general produce broker who was born in London in 1817. He had three children, two maids, one cook and a waitress living with him. The waitress was a local girl, Miss Griffiths from Frankby. Mr. Porter lived in the *Hall* until about the turn of the century when the next owner, Mr. Edward Twigge moved in.
Mr. Twigge's daughter, Muriel, gave the *Thingwall Hall* to the Royal Liverpool Children's Hospital, along with 1¾ acre field and a pony to give the convalescing children rides. She also worked there as matron during the 1920s.

In 1960 *Thingwall Hall* was knocked down and council houses and flats were built on the site. I don't think Miss Twigge would have wanted her gift to be demolished and become a housing estate. However, part of the gardens survives along with the 'Monkey Tree' or rather Chilean pine by the Pensby Road wall.

During the Second World War, Thingwall Home Guard was based at Thingwall Corner where they had a gun turret. One night during the 1939-45 war, some bombs dropped near Thingwall Corner. One dropped where Beverley Gardens is now and another dropped in *the Marl Fields* close to the Landican footpath. Some horses behind the hedge where the sub-station is, were hit by shrapnel. One was in a bad way and George Bowden had to shoot it. On hearing the shot and thinking the German para's had landed, the Thingwall Home Guard sprang into action and Messrs. Newby and Prince advanced with weapons ready. Fortunately they only met a dead horse.

BARNSTON ROAD
Thingwall Corner to Sparks Lane.

The four *Mill Fields* running down from Thingwall Hill to Barnston Road are now under the bricks and mortar of Beverley Gardens. They were owned by four different landowners.

John Milner from Barnston farmed one, which was a good turnip field, and my Dad used to buy the turnips direct for winter cattle fodder. Mr. Milner also used to deal in horses. Mr. Sherlock used to break them for him and he was quite badly injured in that field on one occasion.

Crofts Garage on Barnston Road was completed about 1928. My Dad knew Ernie Croft well. Ernie was a Birkenhead seafarer. His Welsh wife, (maiden name Elias) was a Birkenhead hairdresser and a friend of my Mother's. Ernie bought a two acre field which was a bit boggy with one or small two pits. At this time, the footings of the *Cottage Loaf*, Thurstaston were being dug and Ernie carted the rock spoil to fill and level his ground.

Dad used to go round to Ernie's after work, for a 'chin-wag'. Being a young farmer who had hardly left Wirral, Dad enjoyed his sea-faring tales.

Opposite Crofts Garage, Billy Howard, a Wallasey man, ran a bicycle repair business from a shed during the 1920's. His Father, Robert, ran a poultry farm at Millfield, a big old house built before the Great War and standing a little further along Barnston Road. He also had a fish shop in Wallasey village.

There was a little lane alongside Millfield where Joe Stewart lived in a caravan. Joe was a big smart man. He and his daughter, Josie, used to sell fish from a horse drawn flat cart. Joe was a bit of a comedian. One night in the Fox and Hounds, people were complaining about the smell of fish. Joe said, "My fish don't smell. I've cut their noses off".

Opposite Gallopers Lane is *Woodbank* were Billy Howard lived. The Sea Captain, Mr. Christie, Billy's father-in-law, built *Woodbank*. Billy kept pigs and poultry. His son, Fulton, worked as a lumberjack in the 1960's.

On the opposite side of the road to *Woodbank*, between Crofts Garage and Gallopers Lane are some bungalows with the dates of their construction on them. The Birkenhead builder, Mr. Hurst, built them in the 1930's with second-hand bricks on land, which my grandparents rented from Mr. Holdsworth. It was the building of these bungalows, which finally persuaded my Grandparents to move on.

On the corner of Gallopers Lane and Barnston Road was a tin house in the 1920's before Hurst's bungalows were built. Sid Greenstreet, a farm labourer, lived there then.

At the bottom of Gallopers Lane is *The Farm*. *The Farm* originally called *The Piggery* was built for the army just before the Great War by Mr. Bellis, a Wallasey man.

A battery of artillery was stationed by the railway at Bidston and *The Piggery* supplied the soldiers with pork throughout the war. German prisoners set to work digging ditches to drain Bidston Moss, also had to be fed. The soldiers farming *The Piggery* lived in the farm bungalow.

After the war, Mr. Sampson, a New Brighton pork butcher, bought *The Piggery*. He sold it to Mrs. Coxon from Saughall Massie. Her husband Bob was a livestock dealer and he also owned a slaughterhouse in Liscard. Mrs. Coxon rented the place to my Grandfather, Jack Dawson, from 1922 to 1934. My Dad, Peter, ran *The Piggery* with his brother, Jack.

At *The Piggery*, my Grandparents had twelve cows, about 100 pigs, two horses some poultry and rented 28 acres of land plus anymore they could get their hands on. Dad and his brother ran milk and egg rounds, selling milk from their own cows by the can, delivered by pony and float.

My uncle's round was Woodchurch, Prenton and Oxton, while Dad's was Thingwall and Pensby. On Sunday mornings, Dad often did the Oxton, Prenton round.

In the 1930's Grandad bought a Model T Ford. This made the milk rounds far easier. Uncle Jack then did all the milk and egg rounds and my Dad ran the farm and worked the fields.

My Grandmother was the brains and the driving force behind the family business. She was a real business woman.

Grandad spent most of his time looking after the pigs. My Dad used to gather pig swill from the many eating houses and Italian chip shops in Birkenhead between the wars, by pony and float.

The army swill boiler was too big for Grandad and he had a small 20 gallon boiler built. It was fuelled by coal from Prophets coal round, based at the present *8 O'clock Shop* in Pensby, and delivered by Jim 'Squitty' Burns. Today, Jim's grandson, Dave, lives in Kings Drive, Irby.

When my parents married at Woodchurch Church in 1931, Grandad and the rest of the family still at home, moved to *Sandhay* a small holding in Sparks Lane. My parents started married life in the farm bungalow and my eldest sister, Pat, who lives in Parkgate now, was born there.

My Grandparents could get hold of no more land around Thingwall apart from buying some grazing here and there, as it was all spoken for. So, in 1934, they moved out to *Ivy Farm* in Moreton, which had 113 acres all belonging to Lord Vyner, most of it now under Cadbury's and Squibbs. I was born at *Ivy Farm* in 1949, the youngest of six children. In 1959 my family moved back to Thingwall and in the 1960's the derelict buildings of *Ivy Farm* (some 200 years old) were pulled down. This was a round trip for my family as my ancestors John Dawson and his son Nathaniel farmed land in Moreton from the 1740's until 1807 and Nathaniel's widow carried on farming into the 1830s.

Uncle Jack with the T. Model Ford outside the *Horse and Jockey* inn at Arrowe Park.

Mr. & Mrs. George Bowden took over the tenancy of *The Piggery* which had been renamed *The Farm* and eventually bought the place from Mrs. Coxon's son and the land from Mr. Holdsworth.

On the left of Gallopers Lane before turning to *The Farm* is the entrance to a small croft called *Wood Croft*. In the 1920's this was a holiday caravan site owned by the uncle of the Liverpool Boxer, British and Empire Welterweight Champion, Ernie Roderick. Just past this croft, straight ahead is a field now part of a caravan park. It was owned in the 1920's and 30's by Jack Ferrington.

After the First World War, holiday caravans were put on the field for Liverpool people. Some of the caravans became permanent homes in the 1920's.

Tommy Smith from Oxton, who was a good footballer, had the best one. It was near the gate and close to the water tap. Tommy's caravan was not on wheels and he converted it into a little bungalow for his new bride, Dave Prince's daughter, who sadly died soon after their marriage.

Tommy moved out and Billy MacDonald, a Scot, who worked for the Water Board, moved in.

Mr. New married Amy Wharton of Oxton and started married life in another caravan. Mr. New came from an old Upton family. He was a sergeant in the Great War and his nickname was 'Punch', as he could handle himself. He always used to say to his young recruits, "You might have broken your mothers hearts, but you'll not break mine". His Dad had a nickname too, 'Copper', as he wore a big copper earring. My dad knew them both well. 'Punch' was a building worker for Snapes, who did a lot of brewery work.

David Hale lived in another caravan, he married my Mother's sister, Vera, and they moved to Birkenhead.

Mr. Davidson made his home in a caravan as did Mr. Alexander from Neston, who always kept a whippet.

Ron Kitchenman, a Yorkshireman from Sheffield, came from a well-to-do family. He was well educated and could speak three languages, which was something in those days.
His brothers were both Army Officers and when the Great War started his mother offered to buy him a commission. Ron refused and served in the ranks. He was badly injured in Flanders.

Like many wounded soldiers he was convalescing in Temple Road School, Prenton, which was turned over to the army for the duration of the war.

My Aunt Polly delivered milk there and they met and married. In 1922 they moved into a caravan on *Ferrington's Field* and for a few months they looked after *The Piggery* for my Grandad while he was moving his belongings from Oxton to Thingwall.

One day, Uncle Ron was rooting around the farm and he found an old muzzle loader and a small cardboard box. Unknown to Uncle Ron, the box was full of gun-powder, and he threw it on the bungalow fire. It exploded, nearly killing him, and blew a hole in the roof. Aunt Polly grabbed the muzzle loader and threw it in the yard pit. They had to get a roofer in quick before Grandad saw the damage.

Some years later, Ron and Aunt Polly moved to Church Terrace, Woodchurch.

The bottom end of *Ferrington's Field*, running down to the brook, was fenced off. Old George Penny cultivated an allotment here in the 1920's. George lived in lodgings at Mrs. Hughes' house in Holm Lane, Oxton. He kept a greyhound and did a bit of coursing like many of that era. At the allotment he built a sod walled hut with a galvanised sheet roof. He used to spend days in the hut and he kept a .410 shotgun there, which was stolen one night.

The caravans and bungalows on *Ferrington's Field* were still used as holiday homes in the 1960's. The only one left now is built on the sight of Tommy Smith's. The man who lives there has modernised it and made a first class job.

On the corner of Sparks Lane and Barnston Road is *Holly Bank*, a large detached house, now extended. In the 1920's and 30's, this house, built in the Great War era, was the home of landowner, smallholder, Seacombe butcher and former Wallasey Mayor, Mr. Holdsworth. He owned the land between Gallopers Lane and Thingwall Corner and also around what is now Barnsdale Avenue and the Recreation Centre.

LOWER THINGWALL LANE
AND BASSET HOUND AREA

William Holdsworth ran a milk-round from his smallholding called *Hollybank Farm* which had a Dutch barn and a six cow shippen. It stood on the corner of Lower Thingwall Lane, where 103 Barnston Road is now.

In 1849, this farm had outbuildings, a fold and 56 acres. It was owned by John Leech and rented by John Peers. The farmhouse, then called Thingwall Lodge was a little further along Barnston Road and was pulled down when the road was widened about 1860.

Between Lower Thingwall Lane and the *Basset Hound* pub (where the sandstone wall is), were the two semi-detached Manor Cottages built about 1860. During the early years of this century and for several decades, the family's of Jack Smith and Billy Williams lived in these old sandstone cottages.

Jack Smith worked as a tin smith at Lairds Yard. In those days work in the Shipyard started at 6-00 am and the only means of transport from Thingwall was a pushbike or else walk. Jack must have had a long working day. Jack's son Tom was educated at Calday Grammar and eventually became a chemist. He has lived in Manchester for many years and must be in his late 80's now.

Billy Williams came from a Bebington family and worked as a gardener and made wreaths, etc. He had two sons, Rueben and Dixie. In 1912 Billy and his wife opened a counter in their sitting room. They had shelves put up and brought Todd Brothers the Wallasey grocery suppliers in to stock them up for business. Todds stocked the small shop for £25 and every Monday, Mr. Todd came to the shop to take orders and delivered the goods by horse and van on Wednesday nights.

Mrs. Williams sold bacon, eggs, tea, sugar and sandwiches to the many Irish labourers living and working on the site of Thingwall Resevoir and to men working on Thingwall Sanatorium.

Mrs. Williams used to walk to Borough Road, Prenton with two baskets and catch a tram to Woodside, then take the ferry to Liverpool and walk to London Road where she bought needles, pins, cotton, elastic and post cards etc. When her two baskets were full she would travel back to Thingwall with her 'bits and bobs' and add them to the stock in her shop.

Billy bought land across the road from his shop and started a market garden where The Leas is today and his hard working wife sold his produce from what became Thingwall's first grocers. His son, Rueben,(who died quite recently) eventually opened the shop now called Jonty's, which is opposite the *Basset Hound* and Dixie moved to Chester.

Where the *Basset Hound* car park is to-day, once stood a farm. In 1849, the farm, called *Manor Farm* was owned by Joseph Roberts and rented, along with 88 acres by William Whitby. It was Thingwall's biggest farm. The Whitby's, who had a family of eight children, came to Thingwall from a farm in Barnston, but for some reason they did not stay long.

In the 1850s, *Manor Farm*, now with 100 acres, passed to Thomas Watmough and his mother, Mary, from Walton. Also living and working on the farm were their nephew, Robert Robinson from Liverpool, 40 year old house servant Ann Howard, from Ormskirk and three young labourers Daniel Wilson from Storeton, Thomas Rogers from Flintshire and Henry Heaton from Ormskirk.

Mary Morris was the next farmer at *Manor Farm*. She lived there in the 1880's. Mrs. Morris, a widow with no family, came from Shropshire. The farm had 150 acres in 1881. Mary, aged 70, employed some full-time labourers. Two of these labourers lodged at the farm. They were John Pugh, aged 70 from Shropshire and William Bennett, aged 22 from Woodchurch.

From 1890 Mr. Briscoe, who was born in Moreton, farmed *Manor Farm* and the land round Thingwall reservoir. Before the Great War *Manor Farm* ceased to be a working farm. During the construction of the reservoir, the work horses were stabled there.

The *Basset Hound* pub is built on the site of two semi-detached houses, built in 1916. In the 1920s, Jack Oxton the joiner who built *Jonty's*, lived in one and the Prance family lived in the other.

Mr. Prance moved out to Barnsdale Avenue in the late 1930s and Sid Greenstreet moved in from nearby *Woodfinlow Terrace*.

Sid Greenstreet worked on Mr. Holdsworth's smallholding and he was a real grafter. My Dad remembers one winter in the 1920s when Mr. Holdsworth bought a whole field of turnips on Cross Hill off 'Foxy' Brown. He had no horse and cart and Sid Greenstreet barrowed the whole crop, day after day, to the smallholding yard on the corner of Lower Thingwall Lane.

In later years Sid went into business selling fish and cigarettes from a big basket on his push bike. I remember him in the 1960's, running a paper round on a 'sit up and beg' Irwin's type bike, wearing an old gaberdine mac.

There are still Oxtons, Greenstreets and Prance's living locally. Colin Prance works on Mr. John Milner's farm in Barnston.

Behind the *Basset Hound* is Lower Thingwall Lane and on the left is the ruin of *Thingwall Farm*, once Thingwall's second biggest, with its own well in the yard.

In 1851, Wallasey born Ralph Robinson, aged 76 and his 74 year old wife rented this 80 acre farm from Lord Vyner. His eldest son, Ralph Briscoe Robinson, who was a tailor by trade, eventually took the farm over and it stayed in the Robinson name for several decades. Ralph was a bachelor, but his married brother George, who also worked on the farm, had a family. Jane Lawton, a 21 year old house servant from Upton and 17 year old farm labourer, James Williams from Woodchurch also lived and worked on the farm. After over half a century the Robinsons left Thingwall.

Long before the Great War, Tommy Lamb took over the tenancy of *Thingwall Farm* until about 1920. Tommy didn't see eye to eye with Mr. Turton of Landican. He had a long running dispute with him over a Thingwall field which Edwin Turton rented. Access to this field, was gained across Landican Brook, over a single plank wedged in the fork of an ash tree.

One day the pair met on the bridge. Neither would give way and a fight started. Edwin Turton was a big man and was reckoned to have picked Tommy up and thrown him into the brook. In the early 1920s Tommy moved to the Saltney area.

Mr. and Mrs. Woodfin and their four sons rented *Thingwall Farm* in the 1920's and 30's. The Woodfins were Liverpool cow keepers who did not know a great deal about farming. They relied a lot on the knowledge of Bill Shakeshaft who was their teamsman.

After the Woodfins came the Johnsons, then the last farmer, Bill Booth, who later became a heavy goods driver. *Thingwall Farm* was pulled down in the 1960's.

In the 1920's, the land behind the farm was reckoned to be too poor to feed a peewit, now it feeds a few ponies. These fields have been sold off in recent years.

On the right, opposite the ruin of *Thingwall Farm*, was once a sandstone farmhouse and shippen, called *Woodfinlow Farm*. In 1849, it was owned by Joseph Bellyse and rented by John Peers, who also rented *Thingwall Lodge Farm*.

Woodfinlow Farm was converted into a terrace of three cottages called *Woodfinlow Terrace*. During the 1920s and 30s Mr. Morrison, who worked as a general labourer, lived in one cottage. He married Sally Hignett from *Blakelow* in Sparks Lane. Their daughter Kitty and sons Jimmy and George now live in Heswall.

The Morrison's had several neighbours over the years, amongst them were were the Evans family, an old man called 'Fourpenny', Tommy Tickle's daughter from Sparks Lane and Sid Greenstreet.

'Fourpenny' was given his nickname in Oxton as a lad, where he sold rabbits for four pence. He lived on his own and whiled away the time playing his euphonium. Poor old 'Fourpenny' died in the terrace and Tommy Tickle the butcher moved in, next door to his daughter.

Woodfinlow Terrace was knocked down donkeys years ago and the site is now a back garden.

Also on the right is another old farm, now a private house, as is the nicely converted barn. These two solid red sandstone buildings were built about 1775 with Thurstaston stone. They have great character and are in excellent condition. The front yard is floored with duck stones, probably gathered from local ploughed fields and from wells when they were dug long ago. Duck stone yards are a local feature and are still to be seen in many old farms, paticularly in Landican.

In 1849, John Ralph Shaw, the wealthy Liverpool warehouse owner who built *Arrowe Hall*, owned this farm called *Barn Farm* and rented it to Thomas Jackson with 25 acres. In the 1850's, Mr. Jackson's son, Samuel, was tenant. It had 40 acres then.

Samuel was born in Barnston in 1805 and his wife, Martha, was born in Caldy in 1803. They must have lived in Liverpool when first married as the eldest of their two sons was born there.

Lower Thingwall Lane.
Left, the barn wall of *Barn Farm*, now a private house.
Centre, *Woodfinlow Terrace* now demolished.
Right, *Thingwall Farm* also demolished.

Also living at the farm were servants, John Powel, 70 year old Elizabeth Peers, and Samuel Jackson's nephew young Joseph Jackson and his teenage niece, Elizabeth Jackson, who was also a servant. Both niece and nephew were born in Liverpool.

By 1881 things had changed. The Jacksons had left *Barn Farm*. The acreage had dropped to 18, and 70 year old Caldy born John Realey lived there with his 49 year old Thingwall born wife, Elizabeth.

John Realey was probably Mrs. Martha Jackson's brother. The Realey's three daughters lived with them. One was married, her name was Ellen Crowhurst.

Ellen was married to a master mariner and in the 1890's she lived in Woodchurch with her children. The Crowhursts took over the farm and bought it. In the 1920's they farmed land up Sparks Lane, accessible from an old lane opposite Quarry Lane, now under the houses on the right of Axholme Road

Three unmarried sisters and a brother ran the farm. The brother, William Realey Crowhurst, also worked at *Upton Manor* as a gardener and used to bike it there and back. William died donkeys years ago and one old sister was run over crossing Barnston Road. The last sister died about 1970.

Barn Farm had two wells. One was in the yard close to the gable end of the house and the other was at the bottom of the orchard close to the gate near Thingwall Brook.

Barn Farm is all that is left of the original Thingwall hamlet of the 1850's and before. All the farms were built about the same era and changed hands many times, apart from *Barn Farm* which, for about 80 years was occupied by the Crowhurst family.

The acreage of the farms changed considerably and they had fields scattered all over Thingwall in the last century. Most farms have their fields in sections, running together, but in 1849 the most fields one farmer had together was five. John Peers had one field by Whaley Lane and another bordering Storeton.

Lower Thingwall should have been made a conservation area in the 1950's. Now it is destroyed, like the giant elms which grew down there by the brook in the 1970's, only that was unavoidable.

Barn Farm, all that is left of the original hamlet of Thingwall.
The old barn has been converted into a private house called
Manor Barn and the farmhouse is now called *Manor House*.

For donkeys years, Lower Thingwall Lane, from the brook to the Storeton footpath was like a dark tunnel. The hedges grew over the high bank to the other side with a huge willow at one end and massive elm trees at the other.

Bales were often knocked off wagons trying to get through. George Bowden asked me "let some daylight in" as they say in Thingwall. In the 1970's Dutch Elm Disease killed the trees and I cut the hedge and lopped the big willow. Since then there has been plenty of daylight down Lower Thingwall Lane.

A little further along, the public footpath to Storeton begins as a lane on the left hand side just before *Woodfinlow Cottage*. It is a pleasant enough walk through some of the unspoilt farmland of Thingwall, farmed from the mid 1960's by Mr. George Bowden.

At the first sharp right hand turn in this lane, another branch of it used to carry on straight. This ancient farm track can just about be made out, completely over-grown between two thorn hedges.

After following the footpath through three fields, from the end of the lane, a footbridge across Prenton Brook is encountered. Thingwall ends here. Across the brook is Lower Heath Wood in Storeton.

At the bottom of Lower Thingwall Lane is the white washed *Woodfinlow Cottage*. In the 1920's Bill Shakeshaft, the horseman on *Thingwall Farm* lived there. Bill's mother came from Arrowe and Joe, his father, was born in Spital in 1855 and came to Thingwall as a teenager to work at *Barn Farm*. In the 1890s, Joe worked as a gardener for Mrs. Ziegler of *Home Farm*, Landican.

My Dad always says Bill Shakeshaft was a first class man at his job and he virtually ran the farm for the Woodfins. Bill had three sons and two daughters. His daughter, Lena, who was a nurse, married the son of Tom Lee, the Woodchurch blacksmith, and lived in Barnsdale Avenue until she died recently.

One of Bill's sons, 'Bazza' was a bit of a character. He kept a lurcher and ferrets and Dad used to let him do a bit of rabbiting on his fields.

Towering over *Woodfinlow Cottage* is *Woodfinlow House*, a massive building with bars on some of the lower windows. This gentleman's residence and little cottage were both built in the late 1860's.

Staffordshire born farmer and land owner of 41 acres, Joseph Basset, lived there with his wife, Emma.

The cottage Bill Shakeshaft lived in would have originally been built for Mr. Basset's farmworker and water was supplied from a well in the lane outside.

Liverpool born wheelwright and blacksmith, Mr. Dyson, ran his business from *Woodfinlow House* in the 1880's and 1890's and his wife ran the farm.

In the 1920's Mr. George Limont lived in *Woodfinlow House*. He was a Scottish gentleman and one of his hobbies was breeding pheasants in his grounds, which 'Bazza' Shakeshaft liked to keep an eye on. Bazza's younger brother was Mr. Limonts chauffeur.

Mr. Limont married Jack Hammonds daughter, and every morning, this very tall Scotsman could be seen walking with his can to collect milk from Hammond's farm on Thingwall Road.

When Mr. Limont left *Woodfinlow*, Mr. Williams was the next occupant of this gentleman's residence, and he divided it in two.

In the 1960's, the occupant of one half ran a poultry farm in the field behind with free range birds – a venture out of the question to-day with the number of foxes about.

HOLMWOOD DRIVE AND RESERVOIR AREA

At *Woodfinlow*, Lower Thingwall Lane reduces to a footpath leading to Holmwood Drive. A new house, at the junction of the footpath and Holmwood Drive, is built on the site of an old smallholding. In the 1850's this property, called *Common Farm*, was rented from Lord Vyner along with a croft and part of Cross Hill, amounting to five acres by William Kemp and his wife, Ann. William Kemp was born in Bidston in 1800 and Ann was born in Neston in 1806.

The Kemps of Bidston and Moreton are a very old local family. They were Yeoman of Moreton in the 17th century. The Kemps of Neston originally came from Lincolnshire.

In the 1870's and 1880's, *Common Farm* was occupied by Joseph Brown from Arrowe and Elizabeth, his Rock Ferry born wife who was a laundress.

By the turn of the century *Common Farm* was derelict and the land eventually passed to another Vyner tenant, 'Foxy' Brown of *Poplar Cottage*. In the 1930's the last of the ruin was cleared and the croft was ploughed and sown.

Down the lane to the B.U.P.A. Hospital stood an old cottage built about 1912. When the Children's Sanatorium was down Holmwood Drive, this cottage was the caretakers.

The Sanatorium was started before the Great War, but work ceased until the conflict was over and it was eventually completed in 1921. It provided 40 beds for children suffering from T.B. and Mr. Mathieson M.D. was in charge. They also had an isolation hut there. One lad was in the hospital for 15 years but he eventually came out fairly well recovered. He was a real fighter and was in the Scouts and everything that was going on. The Sanatorium was knocked down and Murrayfield B.U.P.A. Hospital was built.

Donkey's years ago, when Jim Hignett from Thingwall Hill was a lad, he caught a few rabbits behind the sanatorium and paunched them on the back step. A young nurse opened the door, saw all the blood and guts and nearly had hysterics. She thought someone had been murdered, but it was just Jim having a bit of fun.

Poor old Jim is dead and gone now. He lived in Whaley Lane for many years and, his son, Young Jim, who is an old mate of mine, lives in Ridgewood Drive, Pensby.

On the right, as you come out of the footpath onto Holmwood Drive, is a rough patch of land, all that is left of the heathland that once covered Cross Hill. Also, there is an old quarry close to the road, but difficult to see.

The 6½ acre field, skirted by Holmwood Drive with Barnston Road on the far side, was cleared of heath in the 1920's by 'Foxy' Brown. The hump in the middle of the field is Cross Hill, believed to be the site of the Thingwall Viking Parliament.

An ancient road once ran through the field skirting the B.U.P.A. side of the hump and coming out at the mouth of Holmwood Drive, the left fork being the continuation of what was once the original road to Barnston.

In 1850 the original track from Lower Thingwall carried on past the present entrance to the Dales, alongside the house and garden at the footpath entrance. It went to the edge of the dale slope and ran along the bank at the bottom of the back gardens of the modern houses, and came out onto Barnston Road at Dale End.

The present Holmwood Drive arrives at Dale End cutting the corner off the old route.

In 1850, there was an old cottage in the dale called *The Fiddler's Folly*. It was on the bank roughly opposite the back garden of the sandstone *Heather Cottage*.

The *Fiddler's Folly* was an old smallholding consisting of a garden and two crofts amounting to 1½ acres, owned by Lord Vyner, and rented by Thomas Gerrard and his wife.

Thomas Gerrard was born in Storeton in 1801 and his wife, Elizabeth was born in Heswall in 1799. They lived in Barnston first where their eldest son, Robert, was born. They then moved to Thingwall where their other son, William, was born. Thomas and his son, Robert, were both farm labourers. The *Fiddler's Folly* was knocked down about 1870. The crofts are now part of the public area of the Dales and are overgrown with trees.

On the side of the original old track, along the dale bank just before Dale End, was a very old well – the most important one in Thingwall. I don't know if it's covered or filled in, but it was there during the 1920's. To-day, it would be in the garden of the first bungalow in Holmwood Drive.

Years ago the easiest way to get cattle to Chester market was by rail. There were cattle pens at Upton, Storeton and Burton stations to serve those areas. The cattle had to be penned ready for the morning ten to seven train from Bidston.

Obviously, Pensby, Storeton, Barnston and Thingwall cattle were driven to Storeton station.

Thingwall farmers drove their cattle along Lower Thingwall Lane onto what is now Holmwood Drive and down the dale track over the foot-bridge up onto what was then Dale House Road, now Storeton Lane, then along to Storeton Station.

As motorised transport improved the railway's popularity for cattle transportation decreased. There used to be a cattle market at Greasby for North Wirral farmers. My Dad used to use it in his younger days.

At the first bend in Holmwood Drive is the path to the Dales and Storeton Lane. This small wooded area is the only public area of countryside left in Thingwall and consists of about two acres from the original 24 acres of common land 140 years ago.

I've spent many an hour in the Dales as a lad and as a man with my children. It's a good spot for kids to let off steam and see a bit of wildlife. Cross the brook and you're in Barnston.

Stand on the footbridge on a spring morning and look down the 9¼ acre meadow leading to Barnston Road, near The Fox and Hounds and you'll not see a more pleasant view in England.

Look the other way down the Dale and you see a small meadow called *Folly Croft*. It is now part of Barnston Dale Camp but in the last century it was a ¾ acre croft, owned by George Bellyse and was farmed from *Woodfinlow Terrace*.

Past the entrance to the Dales is an old sandstone semi-detached cottage, built about 1880, Heather Villa being one half and Heather Cottage being the other. This property has just been extended and modernised to a high standard and looks really well.

Septimus Francom, the Olympic runner, was born here in 1882. The Francoms moved from Liverpool to Upton in 1870, then in 1880 they moved to Thingwall. Seppy's Dad, Joseph Francom was a plumber and painter, born in Liverpool in 1839. Josiah Francom was as a 17 year old groom, working for Mr. Leadbetter the *Thingwall Hall* coachman, in 1881.

Seppy Francom was head groundsman at Prenton Golf Course in the 1920's. When gangs from Birkenhead's *dock cottages* came to dredge the pits for golf balls, Seppy would order them off. Needless to say, they told him to go away. Seppy was a crack shot with a catapult. He would let them have it in the backside or legs. They would take off after him in a rage, but Seppy being a former Olympic runner would just lope away, stop and fire again. The Birkenhead lads soon looked for a safer pastime. Seppy was also a keen pigeon fancier and rabbiter. He bred quite a few winning birds.

Dave Prince lived in the other half of the cottage. He and his sons moved to Thingwall from Landican where they worked on Okell's Farm.

Dave's son Bill, left Okell's Farm and started a coal round with Ernie Roberts, run from the yard at Storeton Station, and looked after by Tommy Gardner, the signalman.

One of my jobs as a lad was to go across the fields and order coal from Prince's. There are still Francoms and Prince's living in the area.

Thingwall Reservoir was started before the Great War but work ceased during the war years and resumed in 1918. Stone from Thingwall Hill Quarry and from a little quarry dug behind the reservoir was used in the construction. The sand and cement was delivered to Storeton Station.

Some local people, like George and Jack Hignett and Peter Roberts, worked on the reservoir, but most workers were Irish as there wasn't enough local man-power.

There was very little accommodation locally for the workers to lodge in so most of the Irishmen lived on site. They hung canvass over the ends of the 6 foot bore pipes and chambers and dossed down in them.

Bacon and eggs were fried over open fires, on highly polished shovels, with the ends bent up. Most nights were spent having a few pints in the *Mill Inn*, an old Yates House in Mill Road on Thingwall Hill.

Mr. Hewitt was the engineer at Cross Hill Reservoir during the 1920's and therefore lived in the detached house there. Small steel gates through the hedges follow the route of the water pipes across Landican and Oxton to the north end of Birkenhead. Mr. Hewitt had the keys to these gates, and in the 1920's he used to walk the pipe route twice a week, checking for leaks. These old steel gates can still be seen leading from Lower Thingwall Lane, but they are no longer used.

Mr. Hewitt had four sons and a daughter. Jack was an electrician and Ted was a seafarer. His two young twin sons, Bob and Jimmy, were my Dad's mates. Bob was cowman at Okells Farm, Landican, and Jimmy was a blacksmith at Prenton Water Works. Like Dad, the Hewitts were keen rabbiters and had a great interest in terriers and whippets.

A few years ago, another resevoir was built behind the original one. The reservoirs spoil the view from across the road on Cross Hill Hump at about 240 feet above sea level. In Viking times, the view must have been impressive. Even to-day it's not bad.

Across the Mersey Estuary, Formby Point can be clearly seen, and looking across Wirral farmland the massive industrial chimneys of Ellesmere Port.

Every field has a name, and Barnsdale Avenue (price £550 per house) was built on *Lower Out Gates*. This field was owned by Joseph Roberts and farmed by William Whitby in the last century. In the 1920's, Mr. Holdsworth owned it and rented the grazing to my Grandfather.

SPARKS LANE

Sparks Lane is a very old lane but there were no houses along it until the 1860's when a small farm called Sunfield Cottage was built down a track nowadays opposite Nurse Road.

In about 1888, Jack Sparks, a farmer with a long white beard moved there from Noctorum.
As his farm was the only dwelling in that neck of the woods, the lane was called Sparks Lane. Jack was born in Eastham in 1838 and his wife, Elizabeth, was born in Dunham in 1845. They had three daughters, Anne, Rebecca and Phoebe and also a son, William, who married a Thingwall girl and worked as a farm labourer.

Sometime before 1920, Jack changed the name of his farm to *Sandhay*.

I don't know what happened to Jack Sparks but some of his family still live in the area. Jack's nephew who lived in Birkenhead, had a son called Tommy, who was for years the Heswall cobbler. He had a shop down the '*Slack*' and retired in 1986 aged 70. Tommy's son, Alan Sparks, was an engineering manager at Lairds Yard until it closed down.

My Grandad bought *Sandhay* for £750 when dairyman, Mr. Peak, moved to Woodchurch in 1930. The sandstone house had a four cow shippen and an orchard and croft amounting to two acres. The date over the door is 1845 but it was built in the late 1860's.

Sandhay is now overshadowed by the Thingwall Recreation Centre and the first new houses in Barnsdale Avenue are built on the croft.

When Grandad moved to *Ivy Farm*, Dad's brother, Jack, stayed in *Sandhay*. Before Thingwall Recreation Centre was built, Uncle Jack used to let the local operatic society practice in his shippen.

Eventually he had the bungalow *Wayside* built next door for him and his wife and split *Sandhay* for his two sons, Derek, (a joiner) and Stuart (a mechanic) when they married.

In the 1950's when I was a child, Dad and myself used to call in at *Sandhay* with Uncle Jack on the way to Chester Cattle Market. The change in Sparks Lane from then to now is total – from dirt track and fields to a road with housing estates.

Uncle Jack lived in Little Neston for many years after he retired. He died in 1991 aged 90 at his son Derek's new home in Colwyn Bay.

Blakelow, a large brick house built by the Hignett family on what is now, the corner of Nurse Road and Sparks Lane, was pulled down in the 1960's.

Samuel Hignett was born in Ashton near Kelsall in 1812 and his wife, Sarah, was born in Backford. They lived at *Frog Hall* in Upton by Chester when they married and Samuel worked as a farm labourer.

In the 1870s the Hignett family moved to *Mere Cottage* in Mere Lane, Oxton, where Samuel worked for Mr. Langley on 'Mere Farm' and Mrs. Hignett worked as a laundress.

At *Mere Cottage* in 1881, Mr. and Mrs. Hignett had sons, William aged 28, and Samuel aged 20 living with them. Both were quarrymen. Also a grandson, Arthur aged 21, who was a baker and 18 year old servant girl Sarah Kehoe.

Sarah was born in Bentinck Street of Irish parents, who came to Birkenhead during the potato famine, from Castlebar in County Mayo. Samuel and Sarah Kehoe eventually married and moved to Home Lane when Mr. Langley took the tenancy of *Carnesdale Farm* in Barnston.

Two of Sarah's uncles, who had emigrated from Ireland to Argentina, during the potato famine, became cattle barons and in 1904 they died, still bachelors. They left their fortune equally divided between 12 relatives. Sarah was one of them. Out of the blue she inherited £34,000.

Sarah bought land in Sparks Lane and in 1912 she had *Blakelow* built on part of a 9½ acre field called *Bleaklooms*, from which the house may have been named. Her sons helped build the house and on completion, every worker received a gold watch.

Sam Hignett ran his own market garden where Nurse Road is today. He also worked on many local jobs as a stonemason, including Thingwall Reservoir and the sandstone bridge over Arrowe Brook, before it runs into Arrowe Park lake. In the 1920s Sam and Sarah's sons used to work at the builders, Thomas's of Oxton. They used to walk there every day, down Gallopers Lane, across *the Swans* and through Landican to Oxton.

In the 1960's, sons Sam and Will Hignett, who helped build the house, were still living in it. Will was very tall and slim and though an old man in the 1960's, he could be seen striding through Barnston, Pensby and Thingwall every day, swinging his blackthorn stick.

The Hignetts are a large, well-liked family and are now scattered over Thingwall, Irby, Pensby and Heswall.

Further up Sparks Lane is *Rose Acre*, a white bungalow built on land that was allotments during the war, and before that a pig and poultry smallholding run by Mr. Kendall, a printer, and looked after by Charlie Burns of Pensby. Mr. Kendall had a market garden up Seven Acres Lane.

Rock Cottage next to *Rose Acre* and built around the Great War era, was owned by Ned Williams. Ned rented it to Tommy Tickle in the 1920's and 30s.

Tommy Tickle was a butcher from the Black Country. In those days many butchers did their own killing and skinning. He kept horses and store cattle at *Rock Cottage* and had a butchers shop on Pensby Road, Heswall, opposite Sandy Lane.

Tommy was a good butcher and slaughter man. He had three daughters and one of the local lads, who fancied one of them, called round one day. Tommy was working at the time and answered the door holding a skinning knife, with blood all over his hands. The lad turned and legged it. He was last seen going down Sparks Lane like a greyhound!

Tommy eventually moved to *Woodfinlow Terrace* and then left Thingwall for Parkgate.
'*Quarry Cottage*', originally called *Delfield*, was built about 1880 on the corner of Quarry Lane and Sparks Lane and is a semi. The Roberts family lived here for generations. From 1890 until the 1920's, John 'Gampy' Roberts, lived in *Delfield*. John, a general labourer, was born in West Kirby and lived in Woodchurch in the 1880's, before moving to Thingwall.

After he died, Mrs. Moore, lived in the cottage and then Eddie 'Smack It' Roberts. Eddie was a Water Board worker. He and his son lived there until a few years ago.

The other half of the cottage, opening onto Sparks Lane, is home to Graham Hughes, who runs a country shop and gardening business. Graham's mother was a Robert's and the cottage belonged to her father, Peter, John Robert's son.

Peter was a live-in worker at *Manor Farm* in his younger days, but in the 1920's he worked as a scaffolder at Lairds Yard. He was a keen racing cyclist, a sport in it's infancy in those days.

One of Peter's sons, also named Peter, lived in *Quarry Cottage* after him. Young Peter was an old man when I was a lad. His first job was can – lad on the construction of Thingwall Reservoir. As a young man, he worked as a blacksmith at Tom Lee's Woodchurch Foundry, on Arrowe Park Road, standing on what is to-day the *Arrowe Park Hotel* back car park.

Peter was a keen pigeon fancier and rabbiter and a close mate of Seppy Francom. Peter was only just over five feet and Seppy was a big man. I believe they looked a rum pair.

Like most men in those days, Peter liked a pint. He generally walked to Upton for it, probably to talk to Saughall Massie and Upton pigeon fanciers. He was a real character and always had a tale to tell. He said one time his mate Seppy couldn't get a pair of clogs big enough, so they dropped a tree in Barnston Dale and made a pair!

In later years, Peter, worked for the Corporation and in the 1950's and early 60's, he could be seen brushing Arrowe Park Road. I used to talk to Peter whenever he came to our house for eggs. He knew a lot about dogs, horses, wildlife and all sorts of things not topical in Thingwall to-day.
 Peter never recovered properly after being knocked down by a motor bike on the Pensby Road. He died in the mid 1960's.

Pool Cottage, now replaced by a row of four modern terraced houses, once stood on the opposite side of Sparks Lane to *Quarry Cottage*. A few yards higher up, opposite the new detached house.

Pool Cottage was built in the late 1860's by Isaac Getheck, a Master Mariner who was born in Cumberland in 1823. Isaac lived in the cottage with his Liverpool born wife, Ann, and their son, Lawrence.

They called the sandstone cottage *Pool Cottage* because it stood next to Thingwall's public freshwater drinking pit.

Gampy Roberts, Peter the scaffolder's father, lived there early this century. When he died, his wife and daughter Liza lived out their lives in the cottage. Peter inherited the cottage and sold it to Lauly Candeland.

Lauly had a fruit, vegetable and flower stall in Liverpool market. Mr. Tarbuck, the Heswall fishmonger had a shop between Tesco's and the traffic lights. He used to pick Mrs. Candeland up at the crack of dawn and give her a lift to market with her produce.

Pool Cottage was pulled down in the 1960's. The old pear tree is still standing, now in the garden of a modern terraced house.

THINGWALL HILL
Quarry Lane and Mill Road.

Quarry Lane is still unmade, and eventually leads to Mill Road which runs down to Pensby Road. Up there is Higher Thingwall and Thingwall Hill.

On the left of Quarry Lane are a couple of bungalows, *Garwick* and *Mayfair*.

George Bowden's brother Ben lived in *Mayfair* with his wife Joan whose sister married John Morrison from *Woodfinlow Terrace*.

During the war they moved to Caldy, then Mollington and Mrs Jim Gould and daughter Jenny moved in, whilst husband Jim was away in the army. Jim was born and brought up in *Mill Yard* on top of the hill. In his younger days, Jim worked on Hough's Farm in Irby Village, now a vet's. In later years, he worked on the coal and then the Corporation.

My Dad, George Bowden, and everyone who knew Jim when he worked on the farm said he was a real grafter. He could tackle any farm job. Nothing was too much trouble either. He would even deliver milk to the campers down on Thurstaston shore.

In the 1920's, Jim used to give one young Liverpool girl camper a lift to Thurstaston Station on his pony and float. Romance blossomed and she became the lady who shared the rest of his life.

Even after he retired, Jim kept his hand in and I used to see him doing a bit on George Bowden's farm. Sadly, Jim is dead and gone now. His wife is a spritely 90 and daughter, Jenny, a home help, is the last of the Goulds, a Wirral family going back to the 1730's. They still live in *Mayfair*.

Behind *Mayfair* was *Pasadena*, a wooden bungalow accessed via an entry at the side of Garwick.

Jack Oxton and Peter Roberts, the scaffolder, built *Pasadena* in the early 1920's from part of a ship's bridge. 'Breaker' Jones lived there in the 1920's. He was a small man but had no difficulty handling horses and made his living breaking them in. 'Breaker' had a special long shafted cart to harness unbroken horses in, so when they kicked, they did themselves no harm.

Mr. Sowery, a Welshman who worked for the Water Board, was the next occupant of *Pasadena*.

Jack Hignett, brought up in *Blakelow* reared eight children, four boys and four girls, in Pasadena after Mr. Sowery moved out. Like Peter Roberts, Jack's first job was can lad on the reservoir. In later years he worked on the parks and gardens.

After he moved to Woodchurch, he could often be seen with his son, George, and his black and white dog walking the Arrowe Park Road to the *Pensby Hotel* for a pint. All three are now dead.

Quarry Lane narrows to a footpath and leads to Mill Road. On the right is Howards Road still unmade. There are a few bungalows on the left. Big Harry Brown, 'Foxy' Brown's Grandson, lived in one. I knew Harry and helped him on a couple of roofing jobs on George Bowden's farm. He was a plasterer but could turn his hand to anything. I used to bump into him sometimes, across the fields mushrooming with his dog and I enjoyed his conversation. He died a few years ago and is another character who is sadly missed.

Thingwall Quarry is now filled in. It was a big quarry and I spent many hours as a lad trying to climb the sheer sandstone faces. The old air raid shelter on the left has been replaced by a bungalow. The last man to work the quarry was Mr. Maddock, the farmer from *Yew Tree Farm*, Irby, recently a training centre for teenagers.

The quarry was a fair depth and a tidy width. A lot of stone was removed over the centuries. In the 1850s it was two separate quarries but I suppose as the village grew it became one big one. The walls around Thingwall Corner were built with Thingwall stone, as well as numerous cottages. Thingwall stone is yellow; Thurstaston stone is red.

Looking at the old walls, such as the one from Thingwall Corner up Pensby Road, the modern repaired sections can be spotted a mile away. The old wallers were neater in their work, also they built up to straight lines about 18 inches apart. Many of the new sections are just built up until the top of the wall is reached.

Once on Mill Road, the summit of Thingwall Hill has been reached. In the last century, Mill Road was called Mill Lane and Thingwall Hill was Mill Brow. At 244 feet above sea level, it is Thingwall's highest point, only a few feet higher than Cross Hill. Bidston Hill is 216 feet and Thurstaston is 297 feet. A reasonable view of Storeton and Helsby Hill can be had from Thingwall Hill looking over the bungalow roofs.

Here on 'Thinga Hill' as the locals called it when I was a lad, there are seven old cottages surrounded by a new property. The first one, *Baker's Cottage* owned by the Cappers, was home to the Williams family in the 1850's.

John Williams was born in Denbigh in 1821, and his wife, Frances, was born in Ireland in 1820. They started married life in West Derby before moving to Thingwall in 1849 where John worked as a gardener. Some tragedy must have befallen the Williams family as in the 1870's their two sons, Thomas aged 10 and Edward a 12 year old farm boy, were adopted by Mr. and Mrs. Jordan who had moved from Woodchurch into their cottage.

Welsh charwoman, Sarah Jordan (pronounced Jerdon in Thingwall years ago) was John William's sister. Mr. Jordan was a labourer born in Claughton in 1835, sons Bill and Charles were born at Arrowe Hill, Woodchurch. By the 1880's another tragedy hit the family and Mrs. Jordan was a widow taking in washing to support her family.

In those days, *Baker's Cottage* was called *Garden Cottage*. By the 1920's *Baker's Cottage* had been divided into two semi's. An Irish lady, Mrs. Hanlon, who's husband Paddy had died while they were living in Woodchurch, lived in one half and Mr. George Newton lived in the other.

Next door to *Baker's Cottage* is a row of three sandstone terraced cottages, built around 1880, and numbered the old way: 1, 2 and 3. In the 1920's they were home to Ern Roberts before he moved to *Quarry Cottage*, Mrs. Birket and another Mr. Newton. Mrs. Birket's daughter married an Alexander from Neston.

The Newton's came to Thingwall in 1880. Thomas Newton was born in West Kirby in 1850, while his wife, Sarah, was born in Woodchurch.

They started married life in Frankby in the early 1870's. In the late 1870's they lived in Woodchurch before moving to Thingwall about 1880. During the 1880's Mrs. Newton and Mr. Gould died.

Some time later, Mr. Newton and Mrs. Gould married and moved to Landican in 1890 where they reared the young children of their previous marriages. Years later they moved back to Thingwall. There are still Newtons in the area. Mr. George Newton is a retired industrial bricklayer and now lives in Woodchurch.

Just past the terrace and built with the gable end facing Mill Road, in a garden with a laid Hawthorn hedge along the lane and a brick wall down the side, is *Miller's Cottage*. The date over the door is 1797.

In the last century it was owned by the Capper family and from 1848 and during the 1850's, was rented by Townley Medcalf. Townley Medcalf was a watch finisher and so was his son, also named Townley. Townley Snr. was born in Liverpool in 1803, as was his wife, Jane in 1804 and his son in 1831. The Medcalfs also had an employee living with them who was a smith by trade. His name was Thomas Hughes who was born in Parkgate in 1812.

The Medcalfs came to Thingwall from Prenton where they lived in a cottage adjoining the Hall.

In about 1860 they left Thingwall for Irby where Townley carried on with his watch finishing and was also the tenant of the Prince of Wales pub, now demolished. Young Townley ran an 8 acre smallholding. Number 6 Grange Lane (now Grange Road) Birkenhead, was the next home of the Medcalf's, where father and son were coal merchants in the 1870's.

Mr. George Hignett lived in Millers Cottage in the 1920's and 30's and reared a family of nine children there. George was one of the sons from *Blakelow* and the present owner is Sam Hignett, one of his sons. George worked on the construction of Thingwall Reservoir, at Thomas's of Oxton and in later years for the West Cheshire Water Board.

Another house once stood opposite the gable end of *Miller's Cottage* on Mill Road. It was probably the house that Thomas Williams, a farm worker from Upton lived in, with Margaret, his Heswall born wife and their two year old daughter, Mary, in 1851. In the 1860's Thomas became a game-keeper at *Arrowe Hall* and moved a few hundred yards to *Hawthorn Cottage* on what is now Pensby Road.

Alongside *Miller's Cottage* garden is a little walled lane. In the old days this was access to the *Windmill Yard*. Millstones can clearly be seen built into the wall on the left.

A few yards down this little lane is *Lavender Cottage*, formerly numbers 1 and 2 *Mill Yard*.

The Capper family owned this property during the last century and before and their workers and servants lived there.

In the 1850's an apprentice miller, John Scholes from Neston, Joseph Roberts, a Welsh miller and Richard Howard a servant from Pensby, all lived in *Mill Yard*.

Before the Great War and through the 1920s , the Gould family and the Youd family lived in 1 and 2 *Mill Yard*. This was a comical situation as Mr. Youd was game-keeper on *Arrowe Hall Estate* and the Gould family had a taste for game. No more shall be said.

These *Millstones* are all that is left of *Thingwall Windmill*. They can be seen built into the wall of the ancient footpath which today links Mill Road to Beverley Gardens.

Arrowe Hall was built by John Shaw in 1835. It was eventually sold by Major McCalmont M.P. to Lord Leverhulme in 1917. In 1927 it was bought by Birkenhead Corporation and made into a park in 1928.

The Shaws were wealthy Liverpool warehouse owners. They owned *Arrowe Hall* and well over 1,000 acres locally, including *Barn Farm* in Lower Thingwall and *The Rookery*, now The Irby Club.

What is now Arrowe Park, was a keepered estate, where pheasants were reared in the specially planted spinneys near the Hall. Ducks were reared on the lake and in pits. All game in general were well keepered. Local poachers raided Shaws many times. When they did, keepers, gardeners, grooms and all employees had to turn out and try to reprimand them. I knew one old poacher whose father was cornered on Shaws one night and in a bid to escape, shot the keeper in the face with a catapult. He got a year's jail.

Arthur Youd had to be on his toes as keeper at *Arrowe Hall*. He used to drink at Mrs. Broster's pub, the *Horse and Jockey* on the corner of Arrowe Park Road, now the *Arrowe Park Hotel* front car park. Arthur was a big man and if there was any bother he was the 'chucker out'. He had a son, Bill, who went into the army.

Mr. Gould, his two sons, Percy and Jim, and daughter, May, all worked on Houghs Farm in Irby. In later years, Jim married and moved to Whaley Lane, Irby.

When Mr. Gould and Arthur Youd died, Percy became sitting tenant at *Mill Yard*. May married Charlie Frost and he moved in. The Frost family eventually moved to Woodchurch. Their son Charlie lives in Ashlea Road, Pensby.

Percy Gould married Nancy Jones of *The Cottage* smallholding built in 1786 and still standing near the top of Whaley Lane in Irby. Nancy's brother 'Tucker' was killed fighting the Japanese and her father 'Shiner' died whilst feeding his horse in the field where Beverley Gardens is today. Percy and Nancy took over the smallholding, which was rented from John Hough of *Irby Farm*. They also rented the croft between *The Cottage* and *Benty Heath Farm*, now built on, the croft where Anderson Close is built and a field down Lower Thingwall Lane behind *Woodfinlow House*.

Percy, who was an old mate of my Dads, ran the smallholding and worked for the West Cheshire Water Board during the 1960's. He was a gentle giant with hands like feet. The Goulds were founder members of the Irby Club. I often had a pint with Percy and his wife, Nancy, in the *Anchor* and *the Pensby* until the 1980's when they both died. They were good company, cheerful and honest. Jimmy and Percy Gould were the salt of the earth and Thingwall is a poorer place without them and all the other old locals.

John Roberts now owns *Mill Yard*. He changed the name to *Lavender Cottage* and knocked it into one house. John is the son of Peter, from *Quarry Cottage*, and his wife was one of the Cash family from Neston. She was a hard working woman and did a bit of work on the local farms, 'tater picking. Their daughter, Mrs. Eaton, still lives in Thingwall. George, their youngest son, lives in Heswall. He used to work in Laird's Yard but had to retire due to a bad road accident. *Lavender Cottage* is at present up for sale.

Outside *Lavender Cottage* the lane narrows to a footpath and access to Beverley Gardens is gained by a narrow entry. A very old footpath ran from here in a straight line and came out at the corner of Sparks Lane at Barnston Road end.

This footpath was the direct route from Thingwall Hamlet to the *Windmill Yard*. The path then carried on over Pensby Road, across a croft where Richmond Way is, and over Arrowe Park to Greasby. It was very important to farmers years ago. In more recent times, it was probably well trodden by the Irish workers from the reservoir to *Mill Inn*.

During the Second World War, the footpath was diverted straight down the hill, along the hawthorn hedge to Barnston Road. This was because its original route was diagonally across five fields, which were sown with corn for the war effort. After the war, the public footpath's true route was restored, but in the 1960's it disappeared under bricks and mortar.

I always thought it was illegal to close or divert footpaths. Mind you, there's a few disappeared that I know of.

The footpath to Landican from the first bend in Lower Thingwall Lane has been diverted by the owner of the caravan park. A few years ago, it followed the centuries old route along the hedge. Nowadays, caravans are backed up to the hedge and you have to walk down a bit of a road.

The last old sandstone building on Mill Road is *Mill House* once the *Mill Inn*. This was the home of the Capper family.

In the 18th and 19th centuries, the Capper family lived in *Mill House*. Samuel Capper lived there in the middle decades of the last century with, Elizabeth, his wife, who was born in Upton, and their three daughters and four sons.

Apart from *Mill House* and the *Mill Yard*, Samuel also owned four other houses on Thingwall Hill.

In about 1860, *Mill House* was converted into a beer house called the *Mill Inn*. By the 1870's, Robert Capper, Samuel's son, was running the Windmill and family property with Ann his Woodchurch born wife. Robert was a miller farmer with 32 acres and he had his hands full. He was tenant of *Heathfield Cottage* and possibly, *Mill Farm* installing under tenants to work them for him and Alice Capper to manage the *Mill Inn*.

Thingwall Windmill, knocked down at the turn of the Century.

Between *Mill House* and the back of *Mill Yard* was Cappers windmill. Before the Cappers came to Thingwall, the Hall family ran the windmill in the 1720s and in the 1730s, James Oliverson was the miller.

In 1897 the windmill was put out of action when a sail blew off during a gale. A few months later Robert Capper took ill and died, three years later, Ann his widow also passed away.

The mill timber was sold to a Liverpool merchant for £50 and the stonework was dismantled. Cappers 150 years of milling in Thingwall was over.

From the late 1890's, until about 1904 Bill Smith was the manager of the *Mill Inn* and then Matthew McBride became tenant until the pub was closed down in 1914.

During the building of the reservoir, the *Mill Inn* thrived as the few locals and many Irish labourers, flocked there to slake their thirst and wash the dust down with a few scoops of Yates' lotion.

It was closed down due to complaints from *Thingwall Hall* about rowdy behaviour, much to the delight of the manager of the Fox.

The same thing happened to the old *Glegg Arms* in Thurstaston. The Ismay family, owners of the White Star Line of 'Titanic' fame, lived in Thurstaston. They liked peace and quiet. They closed the *Glegg* and village school and had a new school, *Dawpool* built on Thurstaston Hill. With their influence, the railway station was built down by the shore; inconveniencing the locals. Mr. Ismay also paid out of his own pocket to have the new West Kirby Road diverted and cut through the solid rock of Thurstaston Hill.

After the pub license was lost, the *Mill Inn* became a shop run by Tommy Roberts.

The Moore family lived in *Mill House* and in later years Clara Roberts. Mrs. Moore was Robert Cappers daughter and Clara's husband was Deputy Cheshire Hangman.

All the old families on Thingwall Hill were related in those days.

On the corner of Hazeldine Avenue and Mill Road, was an ambulance station which was part of the children's hospital. The ambulance driver, Mr. Davies lived in a lodge over the sandstone wall along Pensby Road.

PENSBY ROAD, THINGWALL
From Thingwall Road East to Sparks Lane.

At the junction of Thingwall Road and Pensby Road are eight semi-detached brick cottages, four on Thingwall Road and four on Pensby Road. They were built just before the Great War on the site of two 18th century cottages.

One cottage stood at 208 feet above sea level and was owned and occupied by Thomas Williams in the 1850's. Thomas was a gardener, born in Upton in 1792 and his wife, Sarah, was born in Tarporley in 1795. They had three sons who were farm labourers, a daughter and grand-daughter.

The other cottage, called *Mill Farm*, was a two croft 1½ acre smallholding, rented from Lord Vyner in the middle of the last century by Thomas Lyon the shoe-maker.

Thomas Lyon was born in Thingwall in 1789 and his wife, Margaret, was born in Wallasey in 1790. He had his widowed daughter, Ann Jackson and his two grandsons living with him in the 1850's. Ann was married to the brother of Samuel Jackson from *Barn Farm*. She lived in Liverpool and when her husband died, she came back to Thingwall with her children. Son Thomas was taught the trade of shoe-making by his Grandfather. He also worked as a barman at the *Mill Inn* during the 1870s. By the 1880s Thomas had his own cordwainers business and his wife Elizabeth, from Upton, had given birth to eight children. A cordwainer was a shoe-maker and leather worker.

In the 1870's, James Maddock from Capenhurst and his Thingwall born wife ran *Mill Farm*. They left Thingwall and for the next 20 years or so the Moore family lived at *Mill Farm*. Thomas Moore came from Irby and his wife Elizabeth was Robert Cappers daughter. They had a family of nine children. Early this century *Mill Farm* house was pulled down but the barn remained standing for a few more years and the Moore's farmed from Mill Road.

With *Mill Farm* already demolished and Thomas Williams' cottage knocked down in 1913, work started on the present eight brick cottages.

During the Great War, my Dad's sister, Aunty Lizzy lived in one of these brick cottages while her husband, Uncle Chuck Wilbraham was fighting in Flanders. Uncle Chuck came from a farming background and lived at *Farm View* in Landican as a youngster. Before the Great War, he worked as under chauffeur for Sterne's, the wealthy German family who moved into *Ivy Farm*, opposite where Landican Cemetery is now, when ship owner James Welsford moved out in 1900.

Just before the Great War, Sterne's moved to *Upton Manor* and Aunt Lizzie and Uncle Chuck married and moved into one of the cottages on Pensby Road, Thingwall.

Every week Uncle Chuck was away in the war, Sterne's gave Aunt Lizzy ten shillings (50p). Sadly, Uncle Chuck was the only survivor of four brothers who fought on the Somme. After his job at Sterne's finished he spent the rest of his working life as a driver for the West Cheshire Water Board.

Aunt Lizzie, who died in 1991 aged 99, told me that when she was a young bride there were some rum lads living in Thingwall and half the village were part-time poachers.

The end cottage out of the four on *the Pensby* Road was home to a local man whom I knew well – Harry Bowden. He was a good bloke and a hard worker, brought up on Wirral farms but becoming a building worker after leaving *Home Farm* Woodchurch.

In the 1930s he worked for Jones and Hough the Heswall builders, on many big jobs, including construction of the three chapels at Landican Cemetery.

Harry had a rough time during the war. He was captured in Italy and starved in a prisoner of war camp where he often had to fight pigs to get food from the troughs. Harry was missing, presumed killed, but was found in Stalag 8, Germany.

His Dad, Freddy, was haymaking where Wimbourne Avenue is now, with George, one of his other sons when George's wife brought news that Harry was alive. Tears of joy ran down Mr. Bowden's face.

'Haja', as Harry was always called, was a hard case when necessary, but he had a soft spot for children and animals. One day, a fair and boxing booth came to Woodchurch where *The Stirrup* pub is now. A pound was offered to anyone who could beat the champion. Haja took the challenge and climbed into the ring. He knocked the champion out, won the pound and gave him a lip like a roll of lino.

Like a lot of farm bred men, he always kept a bit of livestock about the place. Maybe a goat or rabbits or a few hens. Sadly, Harry died in 1991 within weeks of his brother, Ben, a Mollington farmer. They don't make characters like 'Haja' now – more's the pity.

Haja's son, Bob, now lives in the house and one of his daughters, Hazel Parry, lives in Axholme Close, Thingwall.

Next door to 'Haja's' house in *Ninga*, lived the Egerton family who moved there in about 1928 from *Pear Tree Cottage*, which once stood opposite Thingwall Corner. Ted Egerton was a Landican teamsman's son and he worked for the Water Board. Ted's wife Polly, was a Hignett from *Blakelow* and for many years she worked as a barmaid in *the Pensby Hotel*. One day in 1939 Ted arrived home from work to find the house empty and was told by a neighbour that his wife and family had moved to Cornelius Drive, Irby. Ted marched off to his new home none too happy and when he arrived there his wife Polly said, "If I'd told you I wanted to move you wouldn't, so here we are."

Their son, also Ted, served in the Navy and after the war followed in his father's footsteps and worked for the Water Board. His hard work was noticed by his boss, Ron Kitchenman and Ted was promoted to ganger. He retired from the West Cheshire Water Board after 35 years service. Ted was a very good footballer in his youth and played for Pensby and Heswall. He lives in Irby now as does his sister Cathy.

For many years now *Ninga* has been home to Mr. and Mrs. Hughie Hamilton. Mrs. Hamilton, nee Scot was brought up in *The Warrens* down the road, with her brother Dave, who lives in Upton and works on the parks and gardens. Mr. and Mrs. Scot have passed away. They were a well-respected couple.

Chuck Wharton lived in the corner cottage of the four on Thingwall Road and Samuel Peers the joiner lived next door in *Butcombe* before moving to *Benty Heath Farm*, in Whaley Lane, Irby during the War. When he moved out his son, Sam moved in, after working at Worcester aerodrome.
The flower shop on the corner at the junction of Mill Road and Pensby Road was built to replace an old sandstone shop which was knocked down in the early 1930's. The old shop jutted out into Pensby Road and was an obstacle to traffic.

It was once a gentleman's residence and farm called *Thingwall House*, home to the Wade family who were Yeomen of Thingwall in the 1700s. Eventually the house and land passed to Elizabeth Wade.
In 1851 Miss Elizabeth Wade was registered as a 60 year old land proprietor. She owned the fields running along the left hand side of Sparks Lane and Gallopers Lane and also where Heswall Mount and Rylands Park are to-day, amounting to 30 acres.

John Peers of Lower Thingwall rented 19 acres off her, and the shoe-maker and smallholder, Thomas Lyon from *Mill Farm* across the road, rented eight acres. The other 3 acres were her gardens and orchard which she used herself.

In the 1920's and 30's, Charlie Pease and his two sisters ran a shop at *Thingwall House*. Charlie always wore a bowler hat and waistcoat.

The present modern shop is built well back from the original. In more recent years, it was a Mace Grocers run by Mr. Scott, before eventually becoming a flower shop.

Another old 18th century sandstone house which was knocked down to widen the Pensby Road, stood outside Thingwall Primary School. It was demolished some time before the turn of the century.

In 1849, Thomas Cawley and his family and brother, William, shared the semi-detached house with George Williams, a farm labourer. In the 1850's, George Williams from Woodchurch, and his Welsh wife and two children lived in the house. The Cawley's had moved on. Joseph Roberts owned the house as well as *Manor Farm*, where the *Basset Hound* is, and 88 acres.

George Williams probably worked on *Manor Farm* and the house was more than likely a tied cottage. In those days, this part of Pensby Road was called Mill Lane. In the 1890's it became Pensby Lane.

On the opposite side of the road to Thingwall Primary School, is *Carlton Lodge*, a tall brick house with a sandstone front, built about 1890. It is on a ½ acre plot, half hidden by conker trees on land once belonging to *Thingwall House*.

Since the 1890s, the Thompson family have lived there. Mr. Henry Thompson was the Thingwall rates collector and in the 1920s and 30s he could often be seen digging his garden in a bowler hat. His daughter, who is now a very old lady, has lived there all her life.

Heading down hill now, we come to the modern village of Thingwall with shops, a garage and a doctor's surgery. Just past the doctor's, surgery and opposite Eric's the butchers and Penrhyn Avenue, stands *Hawthorn Cottage*, built in about 1869.

Thomas Williams, the gamekeeper moved from Thingwall Hill to *Hawthorn Cottage*. By the 1890s, Thomas had retired from his gamekeepers job at *Arrowe Hall*. Although in his 70s, he worked as a farm labourer and his wife Margaret was taking in washing.
Thomas's married daughter, son-in-law Joseph (a farm labourer from Neston) and grandchildren Margaret Clark and Thomas Stretch also lived at *Hawthorn Cottage*.

A hod carrier called Jimmy Hayes, lived there in the 1920's. Jimmy came from a Thornton Hough family. He was a keen pigeon fancier and like practically all the men in the village, he did a bit of rabbiting, usually with his ferret. *Hawthorn Cottage* has now had its name changed to Stone Cottage.

A few yards past *Hawthorn Cottage* was a red brick terrace, built about the turn of the century called *Hawthorn Terrace*.

Before the war, Bill Jordan lived in one, and the Candelands, Davidsons and Mrs. Thompson lived in the others. Bill Jordan was brought up on Thingwall Hill with his cousins, the Williams's.
Bill worked as a labourer at Prenton Water Works in the 1890s and eventually became a boss at the Wirral Water Company.

In later years he worked on farms. He was a very handy man and laid land drains, laid hedges, thatched roofs and did garden work, etc. 'Toddler', as Bill was known, was a real character and would have a go at anything, including the local game. He could catch anything. He was still rabbiting as an old man during the Second World War.

Reg Candeland worked for Trotters for a while. They had *Elms Farm* on Pensby Road, near Antons Road, where Roberts and Sloss builders yard was. Then he worked for the Irby market gardening family, the Lesters from *Millers Hay* in Mill Hill Road. Frank Lester, a Corporal of the 10th Lancashire Fusiliers and Edwin Lester a Sergeant of the 4th Cheshire Regiment died during the Great War. Frank was posthumously awarded the Victoria Cross – the only man from around these villages to win the V.C. He was shot in Neuvilly, France and Edwin died of syncope in Palestine.

The Lesters had a lot of tragedies in their family and Reg Candeland was involved in one.

One night in the 1920's, John Lester was giving Reg a lift home to Thingwall, through Irby, from a dance at the *Heatherlands*. In the dip at Harrock Wood, a stray pony ran out in front of his motor-bike. John was killed but Reg survived. My Uncle Jack was walking past as the vet shot the pony.

In later years, other families moved into *Hawthorn Terrace*, such as big Jim Wilson, the Pensby Recreation Hall bingo caller and the Cavell and Skillicorn families. Christopher Cavell was killed at Thingwall Corner on a motor bike in 1960.

SEVEN ACRES LANE AND HESWALL MOUNT

Mr. Douglas, the village 'bobby' had a small wooden one-man police station on what is now Howarth's car park on the corner of Seven Acres Lane. Mr. Douglas used to patrol the village on a push bike wearing long leather boots. The kids called him 'cowboy'. If you wanted to speak to him at his station, you had to tap on a little hatch and he would slide it back. The little station was done away with about 1959. I wonder how long a wooden one man station would last to-day with all the low-lifes about.

Where Howarths garage is today, once stood an old garage where the joiner, Mr. Fisher, who built barn doors, parked his wagon.

At the beginning of Seven Acres Lane, where the new scout hut and green is, was a public drinking pit fed by an underground spring, where until the early years of the century local women did their washing. It was still used to water local and travelling horses during the 1930's, but was eventually filled in.

When I was a kid, there was a rough patch overgrown with nettles and hawthorn bushes where the green is today and I used to play there sometimes. Unknown to me, a chimney sweep started using it as a tip, probably my Dad's old mate, Johnny Cowin, from Heswall. One day I went playing there and fell over. I came out like an upset Pygmy!

The original old scout hut was a venue for teenage dances on Wednesday nights in the 1960's.

The Methodist Church is built on a small croft known as *The Intake*. It was owned by the Guardians of the Poor of Thingwall, in other words Woodchurch Church. In the last century, the Capper family rented *The Intake* from the church.

Years ago, Jim Hayes had a flower garden there and Lauly Candeland sold his produce for him. Old Gampy chewed plug 'bacca' and was a champion spitter.

As a lad, I remember all this area between the present Methodist Church and Sparks Lane being a bit swampy. There was reckoned to be a well somewhere near the church, and Thingwall Brook which runs along the side of the *Basset Hound* and under Lower Thingwall Lane, is thought to come from under here. The church is built on an 18th century pit.

When our family moved to Seven Acres Lane in 1959, there were fields and Hawthorn hedges either side and the lane was full of deep pot-holes. There were only three lamps, one at each end and one in the middle.

When I was 10 years old, it used to give me the creeps walking home from school up Seven Acres Lane on a dark winter's night. The hedges were tall and it was pitch black . I used to pick my way to the middle road lamp by the gate to *Heathfield Cottage*. The water in the pot-holes used to fill my shoes. Still, I came to no harm, there were no nutters in those days.

There were nine bungalows and cottages. Only seven of the original bungalows remain.
Mr. Clarke lived in the first one, *High Hedges* at the entrance to the footpath to Pensby.
The next one, *White Gates* is no more. A big modern detached house stands on its site. White Gates was made from a ship's bridge in the early 1920's, the same bridge Pasadena was built from.

Mr. Jackson lived in White Gates. It was an unusual house to say the least. Just before it was pulled down a few of years ago, its name was changed to *H.M.S. Viking*. At the top of the little side lane, passing in front of this new house was *Throstle's Nest*, now also pulled down. It was a small wooden bungalow, condemned and pulled down in the 1960's. The Lee family lived there. Mr. Lee was a ship's painter at Harland and Wolff's repair yard in Bootle.

Hidden round the corner facing the public footpath is *Brandlehow* where I lived. My Dad and brother, Peter, live there still.

Bert Cook, a former Tranmere Rovers manager, lived there before us. Dad bought *Brandlehow* along with an acre of land. It was a lovely spot then – so quiet. Sometimes when I walked down the orchard, a hare would get up. Now it's surrounded by houses and all you see are magpies and squirrels.

On the first slight bend in Seven Acres Lane is the gateway to *Heathfield Cottage*. Built in the 17th century, it is the oldest house in Thingwall and the only old single storey one. It is built in the design of a siege cottage, long, backing onto a bank, with all the original windows facing the open side. Each room opens into the next, with the outside doors at each end and a well outside the back door.

In the 18th century a sea captain bought the cottage for his spinster sister who was of a nervous disposition. Doctors had advised peace and quiet, so the sea captain bought seven acres of heath land for her to walk in.

The name of the cottage was changed from *The Three Doves* to *Heathfield Cottage* and in later years, because the cottage had seven acres of land, the lane, which led to it, was called Seven Acres Lane.

In the last century, *Heathfield Cottage* was a smallholding owned by Joseph Bellyse who also owned *Woodfinlow Terrace* when it was a farm. It was rented by Samuel Capper, and in the 1850's, probably occupied by the Price family who ran the smallholding for him. John Price was a farm worker who was born in Heswall in 1810. His wife Catherine was born in Landican in 1827. They had two little sons, Richard and Thomas, and also Mary Oxton, Catherine's mother, lived with them. Mary Oxton was born in Oxton in 1801, and she was registered as being a servant. Life must have been hard at *Heathfield Cottage* for John Price. Not only did he have a family to keep and a smallholding to run, but a mother-in-law as a live-in servant.

After the Great War, *Heathfield Cottage* was still the only dwelling, and the lane led to the small holding yard about fifty yards past the present gate. This was as far as Seven Acres Lane went.

Bob Cave lived there then, and into the 1920's. *Heathfield Cottage* was known as 'Cave's Cottage' to the locals, and Seven Acres was nicknamed 'Caves Lane'.

Bob ran the smallholding and worked as a hay trusser. He cut hay stacks into square bales, or trusses, as they were called, on a contract basis. Bob was born in Birkenhead and brought up in Gills Lane, Barnston. His father was a farmworker, originally from Ainsdale.

Mr. and Mrs. George Hignett now live in *Heathfield Cottage*. George is one of nine children reared in *Miller's Cottage* on Thingwall Hill. George's wife, Louise, has lived in the cottage since her childhood. Her father moved into *Heathfield Cottage* in the 1930's. Her brother, Les, lives in Brian Avenue off Whaley Lane. Les, a former Water Board worker is a kind-hearted bloke with a great love of animals, like his sister.

George and Louise are old friends, as well as old neighbours. As a lad, George ran milk for my Dad's family in the 1930's. Like myself, George works in industry but like most locals, his heart is in the country way of life. He always keeps a few hens, ducks and geese.

It was George who took me fishing when I was a nipper. At the crack of dawn we'd go and fish the same pits my own lads fish now. Some of my fondest childhood memories are of those simple mornings fishing – healthy and good fun.

Past *Heathfield Cottage* on the right is Cestria, built on land once belonging to *Heathfield Cottage*. *Cestria* gave its name to Cestrian Drive, built on its large garden. A shipyard worker, Mr. MacBeth owned *Cestria* and cultivated a market garden behind, and to the side of his bungalow, but sold it for building in the 1960's.

At the top of Seven Acres Lane are three bungalows. They once had market gardens on the old heath fields that belonged to *Heathfield Cottage* in the 18th and 19th centuries. *Newlands* is the only original bungalow, built on the left. Mr. Kendall, the printer and market gardener, lived there. Today Mr Patterson also a printer lives in *Newlands*.

Higher up on the right are *Sunny Bank* and *The Poplars*. *Sunny Bank* was built in 1927 by the market gardener, Jim Jones, who once had the chip shop in Gill's Lane. In my younger days, the 'chippy' was run by Will Brown and his wife nee Leeson, a farmers daughter from Storeton. The chip shop was round the back, and what is now the chip shop was a green grocers.

Tommy Whitfield, from Wallasey, moved into *Sunny Bank* when construction was completed. He was a market gardener all his life, apart from his R.A.F. years during the Second World War. Tommy was called up in 1941, aged 39. He was first of all stationed in Morfa Towyn, Wales, then Freetown, Sierra Leone, and then on to South Africa. He spent three years in Alleppo plus periods in various other places. When he was de-mobbed, he went back to his market garden. Tommy told me his war service was the nearest thing to a holiday he'd ever had. He used to do a bit of shooting in his younger days, but sold his gun when feeling guilty after shooting two wild duck. Sadly Tommy died last year, 1992, and what's left of his land is now up for sale.

The Poplars was called *The Homestead* when it was first built at the very top of the lane, by Amos Whitfield, Tommy's brother. Tom's sister's dog was a Rhodesian Ridgeback, the first one I'd ever seen. It went missing over the fields when I was about eleven. I tracked it down and brought it back. The Whitfield's were made up and gave me five bob (25p).

Where Cestrian Drive joins Heswall Mount is the entrance to a public footpath, linking Pensby to Thingwall. Up until the 1960's, it was a real footpath with three stiles, now half of it is under Heswall Mount.

The cul-de-sac end of Heswall Mount is built on a piggery. In the 1920's it was owned and run by the Brown brothers. Their father was a businessman and he built the piggery for his sons and set them up in business. He lived in the big old brick house on *the Pensby* Road, by Pensby Close. Mr. Brown owned the land behind, and gained access to the piggery that way.

Graham and Walley were the next and last owners of the piggery. They also ran a black pudding factory and egg packers in Gautby Road, Birkenhead. They had a Belgian refugee gardener working for them, and he grew butts of herbs at the pig farm. The herbs were cut and sent to the black pudding factory for flavouring. The Belgian always used a spade as sharp as a razor. He reckoned it was the secret of easy digging.

One day, during the war, eleven horses belonging to George Bowden, got into the herb butts and ate them. Mr. Whalley was very good about it and just said "these things happen". He was a very easy going man. In the 1960s the pig farm was sold and built on.

Heading out of the cul-de-sac towards Pensby Road, the bungalows on the left are built on the garden of *Louville*, the older bungalow further along. This part of Heswall Mount was a public dirt lane. The right hand side bungalows were built on a strip of land owned by Sid Roberts, who lived in Rylands next door to *Louville*.

Sid was born in *Quarry Cottage*, Sparks Lane and like his father was a keen cyclist in his younger days. As a young man in the 1920's he worked for the market gardeners, Edwards and Rogers. Eventually, he became a partner, then owner of the business including all the land where Rylands Park is.

Sid had a bungalow built and called it Rylands, his wife's maiden name. Rylands Park was built in the 1960's on what were huge cucumber greenhouses. The Roberts family are a very old and successful Thingwall family.

Rylands Park, Heswall Mount, *Brandlehow* and *High Hedges* are all built on the original field called, The Mistake. Elizabeth Wade once owned this six acre field and Thomas Lyon, the smallholder and shoe-maker, rented it along with the 2½ acre field behind it called *Little Two Loves*. The cul-de-sac at the top of Gwendoline Close is built on *Little Two Loves*.

Thingwall comes to an end at the *Emmanuel Hall*, Thingwall's first church. The dotted line down the centre of Pensby Road is the Thingwall boundary, down to Whaley Lane.

The Pensby side of Pensby Road as far as Cornelius Drive was farmed by Mr. Trotter of *Elms Farm*. *Elms Farm* was between *Pensby Hotel* car park and Antons Road. Until recently the site was a builders yard, it has now been built on.

In the 1950's and 60's, Trotters had a home made ice-cream parlour in Pensby, between the new Gulf Garage and the old Co-op, now a kitchen furniture shop. Mr. Trotter's son, Gibby, was the *Basset Hound* manager a few years ago. Opposite *Elms Farm* site is Brown's the pig farmer's old house *Watmough*.

Opposite the mouth of Whaley Lane is a big house, on the bend, called Beech Lodge, built about the turn of the century. It was once a smallholding with a ten acre field behind, belonging to Billy Birchall. Billy kept poultry and a few cows and ran a milk round. Wimbourne Avenue and the Elf garage are built on Billy's field. A shame, as this field was one of the most fertile in the area, yielding heavy crops of potatoes and wheat.

Opposite *Beech Lodge* at the mouth of Whaley Lane, Irby is *Benty Heath Farm*, built in 1732, by Richard Whaley, Yoeman of Irby, hence the name of the lane. Richard married a widow, Katherine Parr and their enitials are still to be seen on the date stone. The old door for loading hay into the house loft, through the gable end was bricked up in 1913 when alterations were carried out.

In the 1920s and early 30s Jack Warrinton, a retired bobby lived in *Benty Heath Farm*, which by then was a smallholding. After Jack left, Fred Sharp lived there until the war. During the war Sam Peers left *Butcombe*, Thingwall Road and took the tenancy of *Benty Heath Farm*.

Mr Peers came to Thingwall from Bebington. He was a joiner and built flat carts in Tom Jones' yard, at *The Cottage* farm near the Barnston end of Gills Lane. He never drilled bolt holes. He had a furnace and bellows and burned the holes through the wood with a red hot iron.

Mr. Peers rented *Benty Heath Farm* and the land up to Cornelius Drive, Irby from Mary Hough. Mary married Mr. Maddock, the Saughall farmer and went to live on a farm near Warrington. Eventually, Mr. Peers son Sam took the tenancy of Benty Heath over from his father and in 1952 he bought the place from Mary Maddock.

Like his Dad, Sam was a joiner. He worked at military establishments and Lairds yard during the war and then at Wimpeys where he was foreman until he retired. Sam was a keen smallholder and kept a cow, pigs, a horse and goats. He made his own butter, grew a bit of everything and bred different varieties of ducks, bantams and rabbits. I went to Beeston Market with him a couple of times when he had a bit of dealing to do and he knew what he was about.

A visit to *Benty Heath Farm* was an interesting couple of hours. Sam is another local we've lost. Mrs. Peers (nee Fardoe from Frankby) still lives in the old farmhouse , but alas, Benty Farm Grove has been built on the two remaining crofts.

Until the early years of this century both *Benty Heath Farm* and *The Cottage*, a little further along Whaley Lane, were supplied with water from an old well now under the nearby Telephone Exchange.

Benty Heath Farm. This old Irby farm stands at the Pensby Road end of Whaley Lane.
The owner Mrs. Peers is seen standing in the yard.

Behind the flats, set back on Pensby Road close to Whaley Lane, is *Heathfield House* built about 1890. Mr and Mrs. Captain William Dobson were the first occupants and lived there quite a number of years. During the 1920s, Jesse Miller lived there. Years ago a market garden was run from this house by Mr. Metcalfe. He grew flowers, vegetables and tomatoes, selling them from a mobile shop. Again in the 1960's, Ambleside Close was built, and down went another market garden.

Thingwall House– demolished in the early 1930's when Pensby Rd was widened

"*Woodfinlow Cottage*" and "*Woodfinlow House*" from the field beside the "*Basset Hound*"

THE LAST FARMER IN THINGWALL

One hundred and fifty years ago, there were twelve farms and smallholdings in Thingwall. In the 1920's there were nine farms and smallholdings and seven market gardens and nurseries. To-day, there is one working farm. The former *Piggery*, where my Dad lived, is now George Bowden's farm.

I know Mr. and Mrs. Bowden very well. They have seen me and my children grow up. Mr. and Mrs. Bowden have lived at *The Farm* since 1934 when my mother and father moved out.

Mrs. Bowden comes from an old Wirral farming family. She was born on Webster's farm at *Big Yard* in Wallasey village, on St. Patrick's Day, 1903. Her father, Mr. Chatterton, was born on a farm in Brimstage.

Molly Bowden at "*The Farm*" 1977

George Bowden at "*The Farm*" 1977. (Greg Dawson junior in the background)

George also comes from an old farming family. He was born in White Row cottages, in Bromborough in 1907. His father, Freddie, was teamsman at *Hall Farm* for Mr. Ball.

As a schoolboy during the Great War, George lived at The Nook, a smallholding in West Kirby. At the end of the Great War, Mr. Ball took the tenancy of *Oaklands Farm* in Heswall, and the Bowden family moved to Heswall to work for him.

Downhams owned *Oaklands Farm*. They lived in a big house called *Pensby House* near *Pensby House* Farm, on Downham Road. Oaklands Farm barn is now *Oaklands Terrace* and Downhams big house was knocked down years ago.

Charlie Reddy was the previous tenant and his sons were both butchers. Burt Reddy had a butchers shop in the bottom village by The Lydiate and Arthur had one in the top village, near Tesco's, on Pensby Road, plus a slaughter house down the 'Slack',(Milner Road).

Mr. Ball left Heswall in the late 1920s, to take the tenancy of *Home Farm*, Woodchurch and took Mr. Freddy Bowden with him as farm bailiff. George and his brothers all worked on the farm.

In 1932, whilst still working at *Home Farm*, George and his wife Molly, went to live in Laurel Cottage in Pensby, where the Gulf Garage is to-day. Two years later, they moved into *The Farm (formerly The Piggery)* at Thingwall, as my parents moved out.

Like all small farmers, George had to take on other work to make ends meet. He used to drive for Roe-Bucks of Heswall, and the West Cheshire Water Board. Mrs. Bowden worked hard too, looking after the farm while George was away driving. Mr. & Mrs. Bowden eventually bought *The Farm* off the late Mrs. Coxons youngest son, Ernie. They also bought the land around *The Farm* up to Thingwall Corner and rent most of the remaining farmland in Thingwall, some of which they sub-let for pony grazing. George no longer keeps pigs or milking cows, but he still has sheep, heifers, beef cattle and poultry.

THE GREATEST LOCAL TRAGEDY

During the last war, Thingwall people were first on the scene of the worst tragedy in the area. An American plane, returning from Ireland with a squad of young American soldiers who had been on a training mission, blew up over Landican.

The twenty four young men were blown to pieces and their bodies, along with the plane and equipment, were scattered in fields between the farm of Mr. George Bowden and Storeton railway line.

On hearing the explosion and crash, Mrs. Bowden and Mr. Bowden's Father, Freddy, grabbed raincoats, as it was pouring down, and a bottle of whisky and rushed across the fields hoping for survivors. Parts of bodies, tins of corned beef, money and wreckage were everywhere. It was a terrible sight. The bodies hit the ground with such force that they made small craters. Mr. Freddy Bowden picked up a head and laid it on a sack he was carrying and his daughter-in-law said to him that he wouldn't sleep that night.

The police and army arrived and kept the locals back. It was still raining heavily. Ambulances tried to get down the Landican to Storeton Lane, against George Bowden's advice, and got bogged down. George advised them to go to Storeton Station and approach from the lane running parallel with the railway line. They eventually took his advice and managed to pick the bodies up. The ambulances drove to Clatterbridge Hospital mortuary, where the bodies were left with an armed guard over night.

No one found out what caused the explosion and the incident seemed to be hushed up a bit.

I have sat in a few local cottages where the mantelpiece was decorated with highly polished brass shells, picked up in the fields where the plane crashed.

LIFE IN THINGWALL
AND NORTH WIRRAL YEARS AGO

In the 1920's, most farms in Thingwall, Irby and some other north Wirral villages, were small family affairs, as they are in France to-day. Farmers needed part-time jobs to survive.

Farm workers were 'Jack of All Trades' – they had to be – but every village had it's expert at each particular task.

People had very little money and jobs were often done as favours on a tit for tat basis. If someone did a bit of work for a farmer or a few favours, the farmer might give him a row or two of potatoes or a couple of cockerels or something.

There wasn't enough land to go round and farmers queued up to rent any spare. My Dad used to scythe 'toffs' orchards and gardens for extra hay. There were no lawnmowers then, and one garden he used to scythe is now overgrown. The house was called *Gilstead*, and has since been demolished. It belonged to Mr. George Stocks and stood in Sparks Lane, opposite Turmar Avenue, more or less.

Cottagers and smallholders would often tether a pony, goat or cow to graze on what they called *The Long Pasture*. To-day we call it the grass verge. They were quite safe, roads were quiet and the people honest. Now-a-days some lame brain would cut the tether or stone the animals.

In the old days, properties changed hands often. Before and into the 1920's there was a lot of sickness such as T.B. and many a man went down with it, leaving a wife and children to the mercy of relatives or to fend for themselves.

In Thingwall and other local small villages, most of the old families were related one way or another. A lot of them were known as Dick relations – they all knew their mothers but a lot never knew their fathers.

I suppose that was to be expected with all the farms and small businesses having live-in servants and lodgers, etc., and husbands and wives dying young in many cases.

Farms in Thingwall, Landican and neighbouring villages which employed three or four men in the 1920's, and before, are now often run with one man or just by the tenant or owner himself.

Years ago, women had no washing machines, electric cookers or central heating. With big families and live-in workers, farmer's wives had their work cut out. They had to be up early to get fires going, cook breakfast, boil water, prepare large amounts of food, (from a raw state), look after children and many other tasks. Washing by hand would take all day.

In the first decade of this century women would have to draw water from wells or carry washing to pits or brooks, as running water was only just being piped into local houses. Then after washing, there was all the wringing, drying and when necessary, ironing.

Simple things like keeping a house warm or keeping the stove going, took time and effort. Logs had to be gathered and cut. With no cars, delivering or picking up was time consuming. Horses had to be harnessed and carts loaded. Travel was slow and at the end of the day horses would have to be fed, watered and cared for as well.

Help was needed to get through the sheer volume of work each day, so people had servants. Not as we imagine so that they could take it easy, but to enable them to get on and run the farm efficiently.

A young, fit farmer's wife often had an older friend or relation living in, or coming round daily to look after the brood of tiny children, while she got stuck into the heavier work. In those days, a live-in worker or servant would be paid very small amounts. In many cases, the main thing was a roof over their heads and food in their bellies. Families had to pull together.

Times were hard and money was tight. People were as poor as church mice and illness was a major set back. With no National Health Service or sick pay, families suffered when one of them was bad. People took no chances, heavy clothing, long johns and singlets were always worn. Heads were covered from the elements in summer and winter.

Once, one of my Dad's sisters was very bad and the doctor had to be called out, and in those days, paid cash. Grandad was only just about making ends meet on the smallholding, with such a big family to support. He always had a few good dogs and the doctor took a fancy to a Welsh Terrier pup he had. That finished up being his fee.

When another sister became ill, things went tragically wrong. She was suffering from fever. Grandmother was mopping her brow with a damp cloth and squeezing it into a saucer when a baby sister wandered in and drank from the saucer. She died days later.

People did a bit of doctoring themselves. My Grandad always put a cobweb on a cut or dog bite. It worked – he lived until he was 87.

Everything was hand-balled, work was hard and hours long. Great pride was taken in workmanship.

People noticed good work and respected the man that did it. Ploughing straight, laying hedges and building stacks, etc., were all a source of pride.

Jobs often took as long as they took. Farmers would reach a stage in a task, rather than a time, before knocking off. The most was made of good weather. They made hay while the sun shone.

Thingwall fields were and still are small, not like in Landican over the brook. The heathlands of Thingwall were cleared in patches and made into small fields over the years.

Because the fields are small, there was a lot of hedging and ditching to do. Using a slashing hook, axe or billhook, they took days or weeks to cut and lay. I've layed a few Thingwall hedges too. A good hedge layer could lay 60 yards in a day. Today circular saws rip the hedges to height and width in a few hours and gaps are wired, not layed.

Dad and other local farmers, such as the Browns and Oxtons, hired themselves out with their horses and carts to Birkenhead Corporation in 1927, when it bought *Arrowe Hall*.

The hundreds of acres of hay and corn took some time and labour to harvest, – no combines and balers then. It was binders, stooks and pikels. The corn was carted to the yard and stacked properly, (by 'Foxy' Brown), so the rain ran off while it stood waiting for the thrashing machine to come. The following year, *Arrowe Hall Estate* was made into the 450 acre Arrowe Park.

In the 1820s, a head teamsman in a tied cottage, was paid about £14 a year and a labourer, about a shilling (5p) a day. In the early 1900s, farm workers in Thingwall and the rest of Wirral were still poorly paid. Wages were only £1.00 a week and rent was about four shillings and six pence (22½p). It was not a great deal better in the 1920's when wages were £1.10 shillings (£1-50) a week for a general farm labourer, but a good reliable cowman or teamsman would often be paid £2-00.

People were up to every trick in the book to make a few bob. Birkenhead Market was a sort of country market in those days with pet and poultry stalls. Dad used to sell homing pigeons to stall holders and 'townies' used to buy them. As soon as the new owner let them out, they would fly back to Dad's loft in Thingwall. Next week he'd sell them again!

A Neston lad acquired a Labrador bitch. In those days, Labradors were quite rare and worth a pretty penny and only toffs had them.

The Nestoner wanted to breed off the bitch and make a few bob out of the pups. He was on the look-out for a labrador dog and walked miles round all the toffs houses to find one. Eventually he came across one chained in a toffs grounds in Gayton. He walked up there one night with his mate when the bitch was in season. He threw a ball through the hedge towards the dog. The bitch followed the ball and the dog lined her and she finished up with a belly of valuable pups.

THE IRISH, WELSH, GERMANS AND 'AKBAR' LADS.

Dad, like all other Wirral farmers, hired some of the many Irish labourers who came looking for work. They were a boon to farmers when some casual labour was needed.

Most Irish farmworkers came over in the spring and returned home in the winter. They worked the crops through the seasons. Turnip thinning in Spring, hay in mid Summer, corn late Summer and potatoes in Autumn.

Before the Great War dealers sometimes brought hundreds of geese over from Ireland and paid Irishmen to drive them round the farms, selling them as they went, mostly in the Bromborough and Eastham areas. If they had to spend a night on the road they would give a farmer a few geese to allow them to sleep the birds in his field.

After the foot and mouth outbreaks in Ireland in 1912, imported Irish cattle were restricted to just one port. Birkenhead was chosen, as the cattle could be isolated before being slaughtered in the Lairage. They were fed on vetch from Billy Houghtons farm in Oxton. Vetch is a plant of the bean family. It was a popular crop for cattle fodder until the 1920's.

Livestock dealers, like Bob Coxon, went to Ireland to buy cattle and sometimes hired good men for Wirral farmers. The Irish labourers came over on the cattle boats.

The cattle boat drovers gave them a free passage provided they helped keep the cattle on their feet. They did this by lying on planks placed across beams above the cattle and prodding them with sticks with hobnails fixed on the end. The cattle had to be kept standing at all times, especially during a storm. Once a beast got down, it would be trampled as the ship rolled,

When the farm lads arrived in Birkenhead they only had a spare shirt tied in a red handkerchief. Their first call was to the Priest who started them off with a pair of boots and corduroy trousers. These Irish lads were hard working and being country boys, they knew the work. They were from all over Ireland but mainly the West counties of Mayo, Roscommon and some came from Achill Island.

Welsh immigrants often came in on slate boats from Anglesey and North Wales. They were skilled at slate roofing and worked mostly in Birkenhead. A lot of Welsh girls came to Thingwall and Heswall areas in the twenties and before, as nurses and skivvies.

There were quite a few German and Austrian families living in Wirral at the turn of the century. Some well-to-do, living in big houses in Bidston, others with small businesses in the Birkenhead streets.

When the Great War started, many Anglicized their names, much the same as Lord Mountbatten changed his from Battenburg. However, after the sinking of the Lusitania in 1915, there were anti-German riots. German and Austrian shops in Birkenhead were looted.

One German, Mr. Dashley, was a friend of the family. He had a butchers shop in Oxton Road and always bought my grandparent's pigs. When his shop was attacked, he escaped and my grandparents hid him on the farm in Holm Lane. It was a shame as he was a nice person, fair and honest.

In the mid 1920's, lads from the Akbar Nautical Training School, (for difficult young lads), were sometimes loaned out to farmers in the Heswall area.

One morning before they set off for work from their school behind the old *Cleaver Hospital*, the lads broke into the camp stores and purloined some boots and socks and then sold them in the village for fag money. At dinnertime the police went into the *Slack* pub and found one of the drinkers wearing Akbar boots and socks. They confiscated them and he had to walk home barefooted.

SOLDIERS

When the Great War started there was a rush to join up. People were extremely patriotic, but also young men saw the war as an adventure. Dad remembers dozens of local lads from Wirral villages joining up. Many never returned.

To boost recruitment 'Pals' Battalions were introduced, so called because friends and relations could enlist together and stay together in the same unit.

The lads of Birkenhead Rugby Club formed their own battalion.

Unfortunately, very often, in a matter of minutes, the rattle of a German or Turkish machine gun wiped out the young men of a whole village.

My mother's father, although too old, signed up to be with his eldest son, Uncle Jack. Families often did this sort of thing. Older men volunteered to look after sons, younger brothers and nephews. Often whole families were wiped out.

When my Uncle Chuck's three brothers were killed in Flanders, his mother wrote to the Queen, appealing as one mother to another, and asked if her surviving son could be sent home. She never received a reply. Years later a stained glass window was fitted in Barnston Church as a memorial to her three lost sons and 15 other soldiers of the parish who also died.

Men under 5ft 3inches and with chest measurements of only 34 inches were exempt from army service. Many small men were desperate to fight for their country.

As the war progressed and the people of Wirral and the rest of Britain saw their sons slaughtered in droves, it suddenly dawned on the top brass that a bullet fired by a small man was just as deadly as one fired by a giant.

A new regiment was formed in Birkenhead, called The Birkenhead Bantams. It was restricted to men between 5ft and 5ft 3 inches, with a minimum chest measurement of 34 inches.

Men from all corners of the Empire and all over Britain came to Birkenhead to enlist. Most were from Wales, Scotland and the industrial north, where hard work from an early age in mines and factories plus undernourishment, stunted their growth.

When the Cheshire Regiment of Bantams landed in France in 1916, French civilians laughed and called them piccaninny soldiers, but they soon proved to their officers, and the Germans, that they were first class infantrymen. They won scores of decorations.

During the last war, large numbers of Allied soldiers camped on Arrowe Park waiting for D-Day. Many of these soldiers worked on farms in local villages to relieve the boredom or for a few pints.

The best workers Dad ever had were three soldiers from Arrowe who came to *Ivy Farm*, Moreton, for something to do. Dad saw them leaning on the farm gate watching him. He got talking to them and found they were Bretons in the Free French Army, country lads at that. He paid them ninepence (4p) an hour to cart and stack corn. Dad learned from them how to stack corn standing up with a sawn-off pikel. They were good.

The Wilbraham Brothers of Pensby, Bill, George and Sam were all killed in Flanders.
The fourth brother, my Uncle Chuck, survived the slaughter.

The men were bored stiff and just wanted something to do and a few bob ale money. Steve Rice, the Irishman who worked full time for Dad, thought they were great as they mugged him to a few pints every night.

Another such temporary farmer from Arrowe Park was a young Czech soldier who became the late Robert Maxwell of the 'Daily Mirror'.

Bradburys of *Top House Farm* was ideally situated for the soldiers at Arrowe and they employed many.

FARMING

Ploughing with the horses dragged on for months in the winter. A team of horses could only manage three quarters of an acre a day. Modern tractors can do whole fields in a day. My Dad still ploughed with horses into the 1950's.

As a child under school age, I used to go with dad sometimes. I'd wait by the hedge as he trudged up and down the field with his team of greys, Sam and Duke, fighting to keep the plough on an even keel.

I used to look forward to the flask of tea we'd share after a couple of hours, in the ditch out of the wind. No wonder Dad's still fit at 87.

The old timers wouldn't plough as deep as to-day's tractors. They always reckoned, "You'll kill the horse and bring up poverty". In other words clay and stones.

Years' ago, ploughing was done in the winter. To-day it's often done as soon as the straw is off the field. Farmers used to graze the stubble and start ploughing when the frost came. The hungry birds would eat the pests and the frost would kill those they missed and break up the soil.

Fields were ploughed up and down hill with the lay of the land, so that water drained off down the furrows.

To start, a ploughman knocked in a marker peg with white paper tied round it, on the far side of the field. He would aim his plough for the peg, to keep the first ridge straight. On reaching the peg, the horses would turn and follow the ploughed ridge back to the other side, turn again and so on.

Fields were ploughed in sections known as butts, with reens, (deep furrows), between, which helped drainage. In the olden days, wet fields would be ploughed in eight yard butts to create extra reens. Dry fields were ploughed in twenty yard butts.

The strip of land round the edge of the field, where the horse turned, is called the headland. Obviously this was ploughed last by ploughing round and round the field.

Fields earmarked for root crops were ploughed first, as the land had to be worked properly for them. Once the frost had got through the soil the land would work itself. The ploughman would then prepare the land by harrowing, grubbing and discing.

Cornfields did not have to be worked so well, as corn only grows on top. Some of Dad's fields were so wet and heavy he had to sow by hand, (or broadcast as they called it), as the horses churned the ground up.

After the corn had broken through and grown two or three inches, the fields would be rolled to break up clods. This was usually done toward's St. Patrick's Day when better weather was due. Rolling in winter only flattened the wet ground and the rain water would lie on top.

A few fields we had at Moreton and Leasowe had never ever been ploughed. When Dad started ridging one field, called *Bottom 'O' the Carrs* by Leasowe Station, he hit quite a number of massive old tree trunks laid out inches below the surface. They all had to be dragged out with chains.

The soil on the seaward side of the River Birket was light and sandy, hence the number of market gardens by the shore. On the landward side it was heavy marly clay and it took two good horses to turn it over.

Dad had two fine grey plough horses called Sam and Duke and a little mare. A lot of farmers were jealous of Dad's horses. They were top notch and he was very proud of them.

He bought Sam from Wilf Roberts of *Home Farm*, Woodchurch, Duke from the Johnsons of *Carnsdale Farm*, Barnston and Kate the little mare, from Wilkinsons of *Diamond Farm*, Saughall Massie.

The old Wirral teamsmen worked long and hard through the winter months. I don't think many men these days would stick the job.

Towards the end of April Dad would sometimes sow clover seed in his oat or wheat crop, which by then would be well up. The clover was sown using a clover barrow, an implement well out of date now and never seen. It was a type of wheel barrow with a narrow seed box, about 12 foot long, bolted across it. As it was pushed the clover seed was sown.

Dad would get the mornings milking done and after breakfast he'd walk down to the field he intended to over sow. When he got going he practically jogged up and down the field. By tea time he could sow eight acres.

Before mowing the corn with the horse drawn self-binder, (which cut the corn and tied it in sheaves), men scythed the headland and tied the sheaves by hand. This was to prevent the horses trampling the first swath. After the wheat or oats was harvested the clover was left growing and was the next years crop. The clover would usually be harvested for three years before being rotated.

Years ago, before cattle cake was available, kale and root crops such as mangolds and turnips were very important as winter cattle fodder. Cutting the roots and tops off, (or snagging as we call it), with a turnip knife is a cold, back aching job, in the winter.

I used to do a lot of turnip snagging when I was younger and when my kids were little I used to snag on a full moon, after work for a few extra bob.

Nowadays you don't see many fields of turnips. Eclipse and Lord Derby's were the most popular. Eclipse are green and Lord Derby's purple.

Moreton Cross.
The row of old cottages which once stood in front of the *Coach and Horses* were demolished many years ago and cows are no longer driven past the cross.

Local farmers grew a lot of potatoes before the war. Digging them was where Irishmen came into their own. They dug the potatoes and threw them into horse buckets, then emptied the buckets into hundredweight (112 pound) sacks or hampers. In the 1930s they were paid between sixpence (2½p) and eightpence (3½p) a hundredweight. A good man could dig a ton a day and they were as strong as bulls. Peter, an Irishman who worked on *Home Farm*, Landican with Alf Oxton, could carry a hundredweight sack of potatoes in his teeth, up five steps into the bothy. Jim and Percy Gould from Thingwall and Jack Middleton from Moreton were amongst the best Wirral 'tater' diggers.

Farmers used to have general rules about weather and dates. St. Patrick's Day was supposed to be the turning point from the winter weather. Milking cows were not allowed to lie out at night before 12th May or after 12th October. These dates were reckoned to be the turning points for cold nights. If cows get a chill, they go off the milk.

The old breeds of brown and white cattle, such as British Shorthorns and Ayrshires, with their long curved horns are not seen in our local fields, like they were until the 1950's.

They can't compete with the heavier milk yields of the black and white Holstein-Friesians of Dutch-German origin. Friesians were first introduced into Wirral in the 1920's by John and Albert Wilkinson of *Diamond Farm*, Saughall Massie.

On one of my ancestor's will, dated 1753, his best cows were valued at £4-00 each. In the 1920's, a good milking cow cost about £30. Now, in 1993, the price is nearer £1,100.

For bacon, the most popular pigs were Large Whites and long slender Landrace. Middle Whites were reared for pork and the gilts of the litter would be got in farrow about August, to provide tender Christmas pork. Black and white Saddlebacks were also quite popular, for they were good eaters.

Now-a-days, even the old poultry breeds such as the Rhode Island Red, which only produce about 150 eggs a year, have had to make way for hybrids such as Warrens which don't go broody and lay over 250 eggs a year.

All the old farms and big houses had orchards years ago. Fresh fruit was not readily available all the year round as it is today and fruit trees were much valued. Apples and pears were harvested, wrapped in paper and stowed away for use through the winter. In the 1920s Mr. Maddock of *Yew Tree Farm*, Irby, used to sell sapling apple trees which he grew from seed.

PITS

The numerous pits around Thingwall and the rest of Wirral are hundreds of years old, some 500 or more. They were not dug in one effort, but nibbled at over the years. Some were dug for clay, most for marl. Marl is a kind of limey clay. It was dug and spread on the fields as fertilizer. To-day bag muck is used. Augers were used to locate the marl. Marl and clay pits had one shallow side with a gradual slope to enable the horse to pull the loaded cart out.

When the pits filled with water, they served another purpose by watering the livestock. It must have been time consuming taking cattle, sheep and horses to running water or drinking pits or, worse again, drawing water from wells for them. Pits must have been a Godsend during a drought. Many pits were dug between two fields serving both with water and marl. There are reckoned to be more pits in Cheshire and South Lancashire than in the rest of England.

Fishing these pits has been a favourite pastime for local lads for centuries. As little kids we used to fish with nets for hours on end. Crested newts were our most prized catch with 'doctor' fish, or in other words red breasted jackies, second fiddle.

Some of the best pits are now under Fishers Lane playing fields in Pensby. The old hawthorns that surrounded some of them still survive. Many of Thingwall's ancient pits are under houses now and some have been filled in for other reasons. Some of the biggest are under Heywood Boulevard and Ambleside Close. Others are under the church in Seven Acres Lane and the back gardens of Wimbourne Avenue, backing onto the public footpath. The *Money Pits*, as they were called, are under houses and gardens from Axholme Close across to Barnsdale Avenue.

As a lad, I always thought the *Money Pits* were a natural hollow. I used to sledge down it in the winter. One big pit not filled in and always dry is *Gala Pit*, in the field on the left-hand side of Gallopers Lane. Years ago, it was alive with rabbits. After the Great War, 'Foxy' Brown cut all the hedges round Gallopers Lane and threw all the branches in the *Gala Pit*. Then he released a bag of rabbits with holes punched in their ears. This was for identification if poachers were caught. It was probably the idea of Mr. Holdsworth, who owned the land.

One morning in 1922, Dad went to get the cows in off *Gala Pits* and found a poachers long net strung out across the field. Something must have disturbed them in the night and panicked them into abandoning everything.

POACHING

Poaching was more a part-time job for some in Thingwall in those days. A rabbit made many a Sunday or even Christmas dinner and many a man's pint was paid for by the contents of a snare or purse net. Hares went for seven shillings and sixpence (37½p), rabbits for ninepence to a shilling (4 or 5p), pheasants five shillings (25p) and partridge four shillings and sixpence (22½p) a brace. They were often sold privately and sometimes to Mr. Tarbuck, the Heswall fishmonger.

Dad used to sell his rabbits on his milk-round and Bob Coxon used to buy any hares he caught. Being a livestock dealer with his own slaughterhouse, Mr. Coxon said he got fed up of beef, etc., so Dad used to bike it to Saughall Massie and sell him game.

Most locals did a bit of 'mooching', as poaching was called. Some made their own purse nets and snares and others bought them. Snares were 1½ pence at Bernards, in Birkenhead. To-day, snares cost £1.70 for ten, purse nets 70p each and long nets £36 for a 100 yarder.

Every man had his own methods at rabbiting. Some were more daring than others and used a gun, ferret or longnet. Others just took a quiet stroll with a lurcher and carried a catapult or set a few snares. Some men would keep to the footpaths and lanes looking across the fields for hares and rabbits with a good dog on a lead. If he saw anything, then the dog would trespass – not him. It is hard to get a lurcher to catch and carry – luckily enough, one of mine does.

Dogs often have more luck after someone has already been ferreting. The rabbits sit out in the bushes and won't go down holes where they can smell the ferret.

Sometimes the old poachers used to take home three or four live doe rabbits and put them in a hutch with a tame Flemish Giant or Belgian Hare buck. The does would be released in kindle to rear litters of big wild rabbits.

Different methods would obviously be used to catch duck, partridge and pheasants. Some used line and fish hooks, others put rat traps where partridge dust-bathed, or pulled fifty yard square drag nets at night, to catch partridge coveys as they roosted in the grass. To catch ducks, poachers would sometimes dig a grip, (narrow trench), into the bank of a pit and bait it from beginning to end with bread. The duck would swim down the grip eating the bread and when it reached the end it was caught. Ducks can't swim backwards and the grip would be too narrow for it to open its wings to fly out. The same grip would be used time and again.

On Sunday mornings, Dad used to see the same faces, mostly from the *Dock Cottages* and Tranmere, heading for the Landican, Storeton and Thingwall fields, with their lurchers, after a free dinner. Hours later, after finishing the Oxton and Prenton milk rounds, Dad would head for home and see them on their way back. Some would have bulky coats, others would have a neckerchiefs tied in a bundle with a bit of clover, a few blackberries or mushrooms showing (this was to kid the Bobby). There was generally a rabbit or leveret rolled up under the top show.

They usually headed for my Great Grandad's old local *The Swan*, originally built about 1849, and named after it's second tenant, Woodchurch born widow, Betsy Swan, who ran the Beer House in the 1860's. Once in *The Swan*, the morning's bag was often raffled for ale money.

Landican fields were more suitable for hare coursing than Thingwall fields as they averaged about sixteen acres to Thingwall's five acres.

Two lurcher men who never missed a Sunday morning coursing, from the Great War into the 1920's, were George Clark from Tranmere and Swilly Stanley from the *Dock Cottages*.

One of Swilly's sons was killed when he fell down a dry dock whilst working on a ship in Birkenhead and his other son Tommy, became head gardener at Arrowe Park. Tommy's son, Roy, who lives in Prenton, was a foreman engineer at Lairds.

What seem to be minor offences by to-day's standards were often quite serious in those days. Magistrates were often gentlemen farmers or landowners and they had no love for poachers or trespassers.

Grandad's brother, Jim, a bare-knuckle fighter and poacher, was caught by the keepers over Storeton *Brick Fields* in the 1890's. It was no use him running, he was a well known character. In court he was asked by the magistrate if he had anything to say.

He replied, "It's not what I've got to say, it's what I've got to pay".

He was fined ten shillings (50p) for being in pursuit of coneys and had to pawn his wife's wedding ring to pay the fine.

I knew one old poacher from Thingwall who noticed how, when one particular covey of partridge was disturbed, it used to swoop up the side of the reservoir and light on the top. One winter's night at dusk, when the wind was right, he strung a long net out along the top of the reservoir and walked the covey up from the field below. He got seven.

The most efficient and experienced poachers to work the Thingwall, Landican and surrounding fields were the Price's of the *Fluke Bone* cottages in Heswall bottom village. They were masters at it. Harold and Henry Price are still alive. Old Henry is 86 now but still gets out for a pint, and so does his brother, Harold, who sometimes took me shooting as a lad. Henry married the shepherdess who looked after Kemp's sheep on Burton Marsh in the 1920's. He told me that one of his first dates with his wife, he took her partridge netting to the *Dungeon Fields*. They caught nine birds which he sold to Mr. Tarbuck. He gave his girlfriend half the twenty two shillings and sixpence (£1-12½p) he received, a tidy sum in those days. Henry worked on the Storeton railway line and always carried a gun wherever he worked.

One old Thingwall poacher decided to have a go at something easier to catch than game and with a bit more meat on. Late one night, in the 1920's, he stole MacFarlane's geese from *Top House Farm*. Unfortunately for the poacher, he left his walking stick (which was rather distinctive) in the shed.

The next morning when the police arrived at the farm, the local Bobby was handed the stick. He was crafty. That night the Bobby walked into the *Anchor Inn* and shouted, "Anybody lost a stick?" and waved it. A couple of bar flies said "Oh, that's So and So's stick". The Bobby cycled to the suspects cottage in Thingwall and sure enough found the geese hanging in his wash-house.

During the war, the same poacher was reported for a similar offence by a more well-to-do resident of Thingwall, who the poacher had seen one night getting more than his share of rationed petrol. The poacher mentioned what he had seen to the gentleman and the case was dropped.

Dad remembers men putting rows of hay seed in the snow and shooting scores of feeding sparrows with muzzle loaders. Sparrow pie was a common dish before the Great War.

Also in the same era, after a snow fall, men used to tie dozens of horse hair snares to ropes and bait them with hay seed, to catch skylarks by the legs.

At Christmas time only toffs had turkey. A working man usually settled for a cockerel. If he was doing well he'd buy a goose for about five shillings (25p).

Using birdlime, linnets and Gold Finches were often caught for sale as cage birds. Bird men often put purse nets over nests of young finches, preventing them from flying, but enabling the hen to feed them through the mesh. Another method was to tie chick's legs to the nest with cotton, until they were ready to fly, then they would be taken.

One of the most experienced bird catchers in Wirral was Ned Starkey from Chester Street, Birkenhead, who worked at Lairds as a fitter's labourer.

Ned was brought up with the Gypsy fairground families, of the Boswells and the Riders, at the Railway Bank Camp in Adelphi Street, during the 1920's. Ned's Dad, also Ned, worked for the Gypsies as a boxer in fairground boxing booths and was a former lightweight champion. He learned all the tricks of the trade about birds and dogs from his Dad and the Gypsies.

Old Ned got into terrible trouble once when he was caught out after painting his well known champion whippet and entering it under a false name at Gorsey Lane dog track in Wallasey. The Starkey's were rum lads but only in a mischievous sort of way.

Ned netted goldfinches, linnets and bullfinches, mainly from Bidston Moss, across Oxton to Landican. Most of his goldfinches and linnets were caught in the winter using a clap net and call bird. Bullfinches were usually caught in orchards when they came to eat the blossom.

In the spring, Ned went bird nesting and took the finches eggs home in cotton wool under his cap, hatching them under broody canaries. Linnets and finches were in great demand as cage birds in the 1920's and 30's. Ned sold scores from his house, mainly to Lairds men.

His son, another Ned, lives in Upper Brassey Street, Birkenhead and worked with me as a fitters slinger at Lairds Yard until it closed. These days we both work for the Ship Repairers, Watsons Norwest.

People are better off now, they don't need to poach or bird catch and it's all the 'go' to be a vegetarian. But in years gone by, people were poor and brought up to eat anything, particularly rabbits and game. They didn't know or care about animal rights, neither would the animal rights people if they were brought up in that era amongst the working class.

Dad taught me about mooching, when I was little and we went out on farm jobs together over his fields. I've eaten my fair share of game in the past and so have my wife and four kids, particularly years ago when I was often laid off or on strike with time on my hands and not much money.

TRANSPORT

In the early 1800s Wirral roads were extremely poor, Farmers travelled on horseback and goods were transported by packhorse.

Thingwall's first public transport link was in 1874 when Mr. Johnson of the 'Black Bull' pub, Neston, ran a daily Neston to Birkenhead horse drawn omnibus service, leaving at 8 a.m. passing through Thingwall and returning from Woodside, Birkenhead, at 5.15pm

This service was put out of business by the railway. Thingwall people walked through the dales to Storeton Railway Station, which was also well used by Pensby and Barnston folk. The trains were fast and reliable.

In 1906, the Mersey Rail Company started a 'bus service from Heswall to Birkenhead. It took about three quarters of an hour and cost a shilling (5p). It soon closed when Birkenhead Corporation won monopoly rights.

After the Great War, Johnny Pye, started a Heswall to Birkenhead 'bus service through Thingwall. His garage was the ground floor of the Kings Cinema in Telegraph Road, Heswall. Johnny's buses only ran to the bottom of Singleton Avenue. My mate's Grandad, the late Tommy Jackson, was his first 'bus driver. Mr. Jackson came over to Heswall from Liverpool and lived much of his life in Radnor Avenue where Mrs. Jackson still lives.

Crosville bought Johnny out in 1924 and when the 'bus station was built, Pye Road was named after him. Johnny's last 'bus was 11 p.m., then it was 'Shanks' pony.'

WALKING

Grandmother's parents on my Dad's side came to Wirral from Shropshire and ran a dairy and removal business. Grandmother's father was a carter. He walked the length of Wirral and further often in the 1860's and 70's with his horses and van.

One day, crossing the Mersey by ferry, a thunderstorm blew up. The horses panicked and jumped overboard, taking a van load of customers belongings with them. It nearly bankrupted him.

My Grandmother told my Dad that when she was a young married woman living in Holm Lane in the late 1880s, she could remember the poorer families carrying coffins in relays across the fields for burial at Woodchurch.

Walking was a way of life in the 1920's and before. Dad also remembers families of Neston fishermen travelling through Thingwall along the Barnston Road to the cockle beds at Leasowe. Their whippets and lurchers used to work the hedges as they travelled along with their horse-drawn flat carts.

Neston miners sometimes rowed to Banks Road, Heswall, moored the boat and went on the ale in the *Black Horse* or *Dee View*. They would often start a fist fight then clear off and row back to Neston.

My wife's father's family were Neston miners. Her great grandfather, Ellis, moved from Malpas to Neston in the 1870's. He lost a leg in a pit fall and was nicknamed Peg Leg. In the 1880's he lived in the Badger Bait, Little Neston, and worked as a coal carrier.

About half the miners in the 'New Mine' came from families from the Wigan area and about half from Flintshire in North Wales.

The wife's Grandfather, Ted Roberts, was a good walker. He was in charge of the pit ponies down Neston mine. In the 1920s, miners were paid five shillings and eight pence (28½p) a day. When the mine closed in 1927, he managed to get a job at Lever's in Port Sunlight and he used to walk it from his house in Colliery Lane, (now Marshlands Road) Little Neston. Later on he managed to get a house a bit nearer, in Buffs Lane, Heswall, and walked it from there.

In the 1800s, farmers and the upper classes were religious. Quite a lot of the farm labourers and smallholders attended church but the majority hardly bothered. Thingwall and Oxton were in Woodchurch Parish, so people walked to Woodchurch Church to worship and Thingwall children walked to Woodchurch School.

The few Thingwall Catholics had to walk to Upton to worship and the Heswall Catholics walked to Neston, until 1919. Then the corrugated iron 'Chapel of Ease' was built in Heswall by Mr. McGetterick, who married the daughter of landowner Mr. Downhams of Downham Road. It was the first local Catholic Church and held one hundred people. The services were taken by a priest from Neston. Thingwall Catholics hadn't so far to walk then, but some still kept to the Upton Church.

In the early years of this century, Upton was nicknamed "Little Ireland" as all the Irish workers from neighbouring villages congregated there. They even had a small St. Patrick's Day parade.

The Last Shift at Neston Colliery
From left to right they are: Arthur Jones, Dave Parry, Joe Burkey, Joe Millington, Bill Williams, Riche Williams, John M. Williams, Jack Campion, Henry Williams and 'Cobber' Jim Jones
The rate of pay was five shillings and eight pence (29p) per day plus bonus.

Grandad, on my Mother's side, was from Yorkshire and Grandmother was from a Rosset family who had moved to Thornton Hough. They married and my Mother was brought up in Borough Road, near Central Station, Birkenhead.

My Mother and Father were 18 when they met. Dad was loading hay to take back to Thingwall, from three Oxton fields grandad rented, close to Holm Lane, where Swan Motors are today. My mother was out for a summer night's stroll with friends. From that chance meeting they were together for 59 years until my Mother died, aged 77. That's a long time to be courting.

Dad missed the last 'bus many times when he was courting my mother and he walked to Thingwall thousands of times. He says when he reached the top of Prenton Hill that was it. Osmaston Road was the last built-up road. Looking across towards Thingwall, it was a black mass, there were only a few lights round *The Swan* and one at the cottages where the Pioneer now is. People thought nothing of walking in those days and Dad would step it out under Prenton Railway Bridge, up Landican Lane and across the fields to his farm. Sometimes he'd bump into poachers carrying long nets and rabbits. Even when transport was available there was little money to pay for it.

Dad used to drive cattle from Thingwall to Mr. Coxon's in Saughall Massie, on foot or sometimes on a bike. Once a cow ran into a chemist's shop in Upton and wrecked it. Dad had to turn it out quick and scarper.

I walk a lot myself. As a lad, myself and many other local lads like Alec and Steve Shakeshaft, Henry Evans, Paul Round, Andy Lennox, Bob Barker, Ant Bennet, Dave Birket, Brian Jackson and many more, used to walk miles over the fields with dog and gun or fishing rod.

In the 1960's, I used to walk with dog and gun to Gayton marsh in the early hours of the morning, wade Gayton gutter and have a morning's wildfowling. Then, flight over, I'd walk back from the tide line, wade the gutter again, swill my waders down at the tap and walk back to Thingwall, wet through sometimes.

Today you see big lumps of lads standing in Thingwall and Pensby waiting for half an hour for a 'bus to Heswall. If they fell over they'd be half way there.

EMPLOYMENT

In the first quarter of this century milkrounds were mostly small family affairs, providing a lot more employment than to-day. Many families like my father's sold their own milk. They had to be up very early to hand milk the cows and get the milk delivered for their customer's breakfasts – hard work at the best of times, especially in winter.

Town milkmen had to buy milk for their rounds. Farmer Joe Broster used to gather all surplus milk from the farms round Irby and take it up to the *Halfway House*, Prenton. The town milkmen met there to receive their milk from Joe and others. They used to wait at the side of Woodchurch Road, where the builders yard is now, opposite the *Halfway House*. Here milk was off-loaded from the farms and loaded for house delivery, by men such as Tom Peever of Rose Mount, Oxton.

The *Halfway House* used to open at 6 o'clock in the morning in those days and the milkmen would start their working day with a tot of rum, especially in winter.

Some of the more educated men studied and became vets. There was plenty of work for them.

When Thingwall farmers or indeed any farmers from out this way wanted to get in touch with Birkenhead vet Mr. Dobie, they rang Mrs. Broster at the *Horse and Jockey* at Arrowe Park roundabout. She would then put a red flag out of the window. The vet would sooner or later pass the Jockey on the way home from his rounds in Greasby, Upton or Irby or somewhere, see the flag, stop and take the message.

Tom Dobie had a practice at Charing Cross where he also had a farrier's stable. Alec, his son, took over from him, then Mr. Firth and Mr. Mutch.

Another man in great demand was Tom Lee, the Woodchurch blacksmith and engineer. If Dad's binder or rollers or something seized or broke down Tom used to come out on a push-bike with a few tools and oil can.

There was no welding in those days, cracks were patched with leather and screws. Tom would get the machine working again one way or another.

A few men made a living by doing contract work for farmers like hedging and ditching etc. One or two men worked as hay trussers.

In the 1920s there were no baling machines. Bales, or trusses, as they called were called, had to be made by hand. The trussers cut hay stacks into square bales and loaded them onto carts on a contract basis at so much a ton for whoever bought the stack off the farmer. To begin with, the man would have to start on the top of the haystack with a long sharp knife and cut out the square trusses, then gently slide them down the ladder. Twine, with a noose on one end, was put round the truss, pulled tight and then tied off. Before string was available, straw bands were used. Then, using hand shears, the truss was clipped into a neat square block. The hay was then loaded and sold in Birkenhead hay market. Hay trussing was very hard work. A truss weighed about 56 pounds.

Irby Village, taken from the field beside the *Anchor Inn*.
Left, *Manor Farm* now replaced by the library.
Right, Corner House Farm now a woodyard and in the road stands Mr. Broster.

There was a thriving cobble floored hay market in Birkenhead, at the bottom of Little Grange Road. At the bottom of Grange Road, Jos Long owned a prosperous corn merchants.

Birkenhead docks, the shipyards, coal merchants, brewers and lots of other industries were booming. Wirral's population was soaring and villages began to mushroom in the early decades of this century.

Most goods were transported by horse-drawn vehicles and the demand for horses and hay was massive. Town horses could not be taken to fields to graze and back every day and country horses had little grazing in winter, so vast quantities of hay were needed. Hay trussers were busy men.

A living could be made out of horse breaking. It sounds like something from the Wild West, but it's true. One fellow called the 'Missing Link' was a dab hand. He used to turn up from nowhere, break a few horses, and then be off again. He was a wanderer and no one knew who he was or where he came from or went.

With Birkenhead and Wirral villages growing rapidly, deliveries of all sorts of goods were big business. There was great demand for sturdy, efficient road horses for pulling delivery vans and carts. 'Vanners' fitted the bill, they were a cross between a carthorse and a pony, a bit like a Welsh cob. Preferably an Irish carthorse mare and a stallion pony, as Irish carthorses were lighter in the leg.

Breaking Vanners was a living. The breakers used to wave blankets in front of them and walk them round working thrashing machines to get them used to being startled. The 'Missing Link' used to take the horses to main roads to watch passing traffic. He would let them smell parked cars and gradually break them for roadwork.

Thrashing machine gangs travelled from farm to farm. One gang was mostly of Neston men. Alexander, Wragg and Weaver were some of the names. They wasted no time feeding the sheaves into the thrasher, as quick as they could be passed from the stack and the string cut. One man always had his work cut out, keeping steam up with buckets of water and barrow loads of coal for the boiler. One thing I always remember was the size of the steam coal. Huge lumps, as big as cow turnips, so that it lasted.

As a little lad I used to stand in our stackyard for hours watching the men graft, while my older sisters tucked their frocks in their navy blue knickers and did handstands against the barn walls. Happy days!

Apart from farm-related work and gardening, there was not a lot of regular employment in the villages of North Wirral.

Quite a few men from Thingwall, Pensby, Irby and Heswall found work on the West Cheshire Water Board, laying water mains as new property sprang up in the 1920's. The depot was in Gills Lane, Barnston on the corner of Thorncroft Drive.

One or two men worked at Prenton Water Works at the bottom of Water Park Road. Mr. Barton and his four sons, Arthur, Edgar, Jim and Harold, ran the Water Works. Jim was tragically killed when he fell down the well. There are still members of the Barton family living locally.

With the increase in motor traffic and new property being built, roads had to be widened and improved. Roadworks became quite an employer of men in the late 1920s and 30s.

In 1929 the World Scout Jamboree, held at Arrowe Park, was attended by over 30,000 scouts from all over the world. In preparation for extra traffic and V.I.Ps, Woodchurch Road, from Birkenhead to Arrowe Park, was widened and improved with a coat of MacAdam. A lot of team owners were employed to cart the MacAdam and dump it in rucks along the road, for the road gangs to spread.

The next road to be widened and improved was Arrowe Park Road, from Arrowe Park Gates to Thingwall Corner. Thingwall Corner was very sharp and two 'buses could not pass, so *Pear Tree Cottage* was pulled down and the sandstone wall opposite was taken down and rebuilt further back where it is today.

Huge rocks from the Mersey Tunnel excavations were dumped in the road and gangs of men broke them into hardcore with sledgehammers. After the hardcore was spread, it was coated with concrete and tamped flat, using huge planks with wooden handles nailed to them.

Everything was done by hand, there were no cement mixers, jack hammers or dumper trucks. Pensby Road was also widened and improved in the early 1930s.

There were no flush toilets or bin men in Thingwall, or neighbouring villages, in the first decades of this century. The primitive outside toilets were called ash pits, because fire grate ashes were thrown in, to cover and soak up the human waste or 'night soil' as it was called.

Gathering and carting away 'night soil' provided men with work. 'Wacko' Jones of *The Cottage* farm, Gills Lane, used to gather night soil mostly from New Town and Pensby and spread it for fertilizer, on the fields he rented round Thingwall Reservoir. Bottles and jars etc., were often dumped in old marl pits.

The night soil from Oxton and Tranmere was carted by council workers and dumped in pits near the flat lanes of Oxton, many where the Holmlands Estate is today. Dad remembers one occasion, when a horse was backing a big load into a pit, it carried away and dragged the horse under and drowned it.
A few years ago when we had a severe drought and several pits dried up, my Nephew, Dave Edwards, from Pensby, dug out quite a collection of Victorian bottles. Also, in the same vicinity, my brother, Peter, found two pieces of a mug commemorating the assassination of President Garfield of America, in 1881. On ploughed fields all over Wirral bits of broken cups and plates etc., can be found, from the days of night soil spreading

Men from all North Wirral villages, including Thingwall, have for centuries been sailors, or mariners as they were called years ago.

In the 17th and 18th centuries, many sailed from Parkgate and the old Thurstaston port of *Dawpool*, to Dublin and Europe and others from Liverpool worldwide. In the early 1700's two of my ancestors were mariners – John Dawson from Thurstaston and Simon Dawson from Irby, who was buried at sea in 1725.

Wirral ports, and the River Dee, were very busy. Thousands of troops sailed from Hoylake and Hilbre to Ireland with William of Orange, to fight the Battle of the Boyne. His point of embarkation is still commemorated with the name, *Kings Gap*.

I've been told old tales of Royal Navy press gangs visiting Parkgate, *Dawpool* and Hoylake, looking for 'recruits' and of local sailors and fishermen, hiding out in the Dungeons at Thurstaston, 'till they saw the sails of the frigates leave the Dee.

My Grandmother's brother, Uncle Willie, was a mariner. He sailed all over the world from the 1870's to the 90's, sometimes from Birkenhead, Wirral to Birkenhead, Australia.

He sailed on a passenger ship bound for Australia on one occasion. Passengers were all over the deck when the ship suddenly lurched and a lady dropped her babe in arms over the side. Willie, who was painting on the upper deck, dived over the side, swam to the child and held it up until a lifeboat could be launched to complete the rescue.

When he got back aboard, the lady, who was quite well off, took off all her rings and jewellery and gave it to him. Willie was a rich man for a while but he was a terrible man for the drink and soon frittered his small fortune away.

Regular money for months at a time and tales of exotic places, drew many men to the sea. Until very recently, Birkenhead and Liverpool were extremely busy ports and many local families had one or two seafarer's amongst them. I've done a few trips myself.

A Bobby's job was good regular work. In 1919 the police went on strike. Serious looting, vandalism and rioting started in Birkenhead, when on August 1st, 114 Sergeants and Constables withdrew their services. Special constables were called out and 500 troops of the Scots Greys arrived in town.

All striking policemen were sacked. Men from all over Wirral and Lancashire travelled to Birkenhead to apply for the vacant jobs.

My Uncle Dick and his brothers came over from their smallholding in West Houghton, Lancashire, to join the force.

Hundreds of men lay on the grass opposite the Town Hall waiting for it to open for interviews.

Uncle Dick was one of the lucky ones and started as a constable, based at Slatey Road Police Station, which was unfortunately bombed during the last War. He liked the job but the only drawback was that his sergeant was a stickler and insisted he recorded every detail in his notebook and like myself, Uncle Dick was no scholar.

One morning he said to my Grandad, "I nearly ruptured myself on duty last night, Jack". "How did you manage that?" asked Grandad." I came across this half- dead horse in Tollemache Road" replied Uncle Dick, "and I had to drag it into Park Road". "What the hell for?" enquired Grandad. "Cos I couldn't spell Tollemache" moaned Uncle Dick.

To make ends meet many women became skivvies or laundresses and took in washing from better off people in the area or from men who lived alone.

In the 1920's, some local women took in washing from toffs around Claughton and Oxton. Mr. John Moore, from Rocky Lane, Heswall took them every week in his wagon to drop the clean laundry off, get paid and pick up the next batch of washing. Then he'd run the women to Birkenhead market for their shopping, before dropping them all off home with their baggage.

SPORT

Years ago the simple down to earth sports were the only ones the working man could watch or partake in. Fishing, shooting, dog and horse racing, football, bowles and boxing were all very popular.

In the early 1800s the Yeomen farmers all kept greyhounds for coursing and arranged meets on each other's land. Shooting and coursing were still very popular pursuits in our local villages during the 1920s and 30s.

Gorsey Lane dog track in Wallasey drew large crowds.

Men worked hard and played hard when they could. With no television, transport or enough money to go places, the local pubs and sports teams were well supported.

On Saturdays, Dad and his mates used to rush to get through the farm work, so that they could go and watch 'Dixie' Dean play for Pensby.

Billy Dean ran milk for Burgess' of *Arrowe House Farm*, where Champion Spark Plugs is now. He lived in Birkenhead and when Pensby signed him, he used to bike it down to play on a pitch behind what is now the *8 O'Clock Shop* on Pensby Road.

Big crowds used to watch the local matches in those days. It was the only football most of them saw.

Dixie used to practice by running along side brick walls, kicking a ball against them at different angles. He was only fourteen when he signed for Pensby in 1921, and was snaffled by Tranmere at the age of sixteen. The fee was reckoned to be a new football kit for the Pensby team.

In later years Coles chicken hatchery was built on the old Pensby pitch.

Bowls was becoming popular at the beginning of the century. Fields were flayed of turf to provide instant greens. The fields around Harrocks Wood, in Irby, were flayed by Jack Maddock, and the turf was sent to Wallasey for laying out parks and greens.

Boxing was always very popular in Wirral. With the vast majority of men engaged in manual labour, strength, fitness and fighting prowess were always talking points.

Hilbre Island was sometimes the venue for bare knuckle fights early in the last century and for cock fights they reckon. When the tide was in, participants were safe from interference from the law and the old pub that was on the island probably did a roaring trade also.

At the turn of the century hard cases like Grandad's brother, Jim, used to fight bare knuckle for bets, often outside *The Swan*.

In the 1920s, the Heswall lads used to organise teams to box lads from the 'Akbar'. One or two of the Akbar lads were black, (the first black people the vast majority of Heswall folk had seen), and a couple of local lads wanted to be the first to box them.
Old Jack Price, now sadly dead and gone, told me that he was one of the locals who fought one of the Liverpool negroes. They proved to be very tough and skilful boxers. At the next tournament it was a lot harder to find someone willing to take them on.

In more recent times, Birkenhead haymarket loft was eventually turned into a boxing club, my first.

OLD SAYINGS AND AMUSING CHARACTERS

The old West Wirral accent is no longer heard in Thingwall like it was thirty or forty years ago. You don't hear shouts from the old timers to gangs of kids asking, "Where are yay lot bound for?" and "How are yoe going on owd'n".

Some of the farm workers used to say some funny things and the old sayings used to amuse me. Such as when something was high, they'd say "That's a tidy depth up" and when new boots rubbed, they'd say, "Leave 'em off for a day or two till ye get used to 'em".

When it looked like bad weather was coming, someone would say, "If you can see Wales its going to rain and if you can't see Wales it is raining."

When working in the fields on a winter's day, comedians like Grandad's cousin, George Saxon, from Frankby, used to say "Shut that bloody gate, it's blowing a gale in here!"

My Grandad used to get up about 4 o'clock in the morning, and if anyone asked him the time after 7 o'clock, he'd say, "dinner time".

A few days after putting rat poison down, my Dad asked old McGahan the Irishman to get a couple of hundredweight of corn down out of the granary. McGahan shifted some sacks and found a number of rat's corpses. He said "Sure, the place is alive with dead rats".

Tommy Luckan, went home to Ireland for the winter and when he came back he mentioned his family had been very ill. One of the farm workers said "I believe the family was off colour Tommy". "Aye," Tommy replied, "sure they were all terrible bad, even the cat was as sick as a dog".

When Owen, another Irishman, said he was going home for Christmas to see his family, George Bowden asked him how many kids he had. He replied, five or six or seven.

Once, in about 1959, I was coming down Seven Acres Lane with my fishing rod and bucket when old Peter Roberts saw me. "All reet young'n, where've yoe been and what's in the bucket ?" he asked. "*Wacko's Pits* and a couple of rudd" said I. "Let's have a decko" he muttered. "Call them rudd", he said. "I was fishing *Wackos* one time and I caught a proper rudd, it was that big, when I dragged it out, the water dropped a foot". Then he winked and walked off chuckling.

Kirk Okell, the farmer, was convinced old Fred Jones who worked for him was over 65. Every time Kirk asked the old tractor man how old he was, Fred just said, "Getting on". Fred was found dead in bed at his house in Hesketh Drive, Heswall a few years ago.

An old saying farmers used, was "two moons in May, bad fruit and bad hay". In other words, if there was a full moon at the beginning of May and one at the end, there would be wind and rain all summer.

If a local got into bother, their family rallied round and kept it quiet and the old Wirral saying was repeated, "Say nowt and keep yer own counsel". When people were on hard times neighbours helped. As my Dad always says, a little help is worth a lot of pity.

A well-educated lady fell on hard times when her sea captain husband disappeared at sea during the Great War. She had to take in sewing and knitting, and ran up quite a milk and egg bill with Grandad. He saw to it that the deliveries were kept up as he'd heard about her dilemma. Eventually she had to get out of her house and being of a generation that was brought up to have pride, she wanted to settle her bill and it was agreed that Grandad would have her garden shed.

All the women of Holm Lane, Oxton, used to bake cakes and pies for Billy Houghton as his wife was in a bathchair. Billy's farm, built by the Earl of Shrewsbury, was the most awkward set up. The farm buildings were up Holm Lane, and he was given a house on Woodchurch Road, near the top of Prenton Hill. It was last in a row of twelve semi's running up the hill from the *Swan Hotel* and to-day it is number 478 Woodchurch Road.

Farmers are not people to be kidded or beat about the bush. Anyone not trusted or disliked soon got the message.

Old Mr. Holland the cattle dealer, and Liverpool corn and Hay dealer, Albert Backhouse, were always welcome as they gave a fair price and didn't moan or haggle. Old Holland was ancient in the early 1950's. He always came dressed in a bowler hat and smart suit with a waistcoat and 'Albert'. He dropped me a silver shilling once. I'll never forget it. It was like Christmas. You were lucky if you saw a three-penny joey in those days.

Pierre the onion seller was a welcome visitor years ago, he always gave value for money.

Gypsies used to come round the farms and do a bit of palm-reading and odd jobs etc. They were real gypsies, like the Smith's and Taylors, not the scruffs you see to-day with wirelesses blaring. Some came from the gypsy camp in Green Lane, Tranmere, and often camped at Fishers Lane or Telegraph Road, Thurstaston. They were always on the look out for good horse grazing and when the last farm light went out, they'd let their ponies loose on the nearest good pasture field. Before first light, they'd have the ponies tethered back at the caravan before anyone was about. The gypsies never really did any harm, but some of the locals got up to a bit of mischief when the gypsies came and blamed it on them.

I used to enjoy a pint in the 1960's listening to the local old age pensioners. Most are dead and gone now. I've been told many an interesting tale in *The Pensby*, *Anchor* and in pubs in Heswall and Neston.

My Dad, George Bowden, and one or two more of their age group, are the last of a generation who farmed in Thingwall's last years as a truly rural village, living a real country life.

Tales and folk-law from all over North Wirral, spanning over 200 years, have passed down through our family. Some information is quite accurate, some not so.

My Grandfather's Grandfather, John Dawson, was born on his father's farm in Irby in 1800. When he was born, Birkenhead was a village of only one hundred and ten souls and the nearest post office or butchers shop was in Neston. John worked as a wheelwright in 1821 and there were still only 200 inhabitants. Ten years later, when John was a 31 year old joiner working at Lairds Shipyard and living in Chester Street, Birkenhead's population had increased over 12 fold to 2,569.

At 41 he was tenant of a small farm in Oxton and Birkenhead's population had soared to 8,223. They were living in 1,270 houses with a further 91 houses in various stages of construction. Only a quarter of the people were from Cheshire. Most were from Ireland, Wales, Lancashire, Shropshire and Scotland.

John saw a picturesque dale, with a brook running down it's centre into Tranmere Pool, turn into part of the town. By the time he died in *Elder Cottage*, Salem View, Oxton in 1874, the sloping sides of the dale were built up with the terraced houses of Tranmere and Oxton. The bottom of the dale called Happy Valley had become Borough Road. The brook, known as *The Rubicon* was piped under Borough Road into the Mersey. Tranmere Pool was no longer a rocky inlet, but Lairds Basin, and Birkenhead's population had risen to over 70,000.

In one man's lifetime a small Wirral village had grown into a huge town, with it's own docks, shipyards, factories and the third biggest square in Europe.

Birkenhead Woodside Ferry c1936 WPC 64

UNUSUAL FACTS NOTED

Having waded through scores of Victorian records, one thing struck me as odd. Queen Victoria was our longest reigning monarch. She was on the throne for sixty four years, yet I never came across one single female named after her.

Below is an unusual record of a death from St. Mary's Church records (The Priory), Birkenhead. 7/April/1777.

Martha Lacy, aged 102, a remarkable liver. Mother of nineteen children and was able to work until within one month of her death. Never remembered sickness until one and a half years ago. Had a retentive memory from King James II's time till George II's accession. Afterwards she remembered little of public recurrences tho' she retained her rational faculties to the last.

THINGWALL COMMONS AND WOODLAND

Thingwall is badly off for public open spaces. Pensby, Heswall, Irby and surrounding villages have parks and playing fields. Thingwall only has a couple of acres of land open to the public now, down the dales off Holmwood Drive.

In years gone by, the gentry took all the best land and left the peasants some of the poorer land to share as common grazing etc. This was true in Thingwall.

In 1849, there were 24 acres of common land in Thingwall. One acre was where the drinking pit was, around the scout hut in Seven Acres Lane. Three and a half acres were up Quarry Lane, where the quarry was, and just over nineteen acres were around Holmwood Drive.

On these areas, Thingwall people were allowed to quarry, gather fire wood and graze and water their livestock.

Common rights in Thingwall, were abolished in 1868 and it must have been a blow to the villagers, particularly the cottagers and smallholders. Today practically all the original common land is now in private hands.

The individual's gain is the community's loss. Years ago a football pitch was cut out of the heathland down the dales for use by people at Barnston Dale camp, once a farm. This area, along with *Folly Croft*, down below in the dale are part of the camp, but at least they are not built on and are available to the community.

By the 1920's all farm heathland in Thingwall had been cleared and improved. The rent was about £1.10 shillings (£1-50) an acre. Land rent rose to £5.00 an acre in the 1960's. Now, in 1993, Thingwall farmland is £73.00 an acre and rises every three years.

About half of the land area of Thingwall is built on. The other half is Water Board, pony grazing and farmland. Building has stopped apart from a bit of in-filling.

Thingwall is poorly off for woodland. The only reasonable area of woodland is largely of hand planted pine trees in the B.U.P.A hospital grounds. There are also a couple of hand planted groves which were once in the grounds of *Thingwall Hall* and are now part of the Thingwall Corner estate.

Down the dales, off Holmwood Drive are a couple of acres of natural woodland. Apart from that there is only one natural small spinney of oak trees. The spinney is at *Wacko's pits* close to Thingwall Reservoir. The Barnston / Thingwall boundary ditch is one side and old marl pits are on the other.

These twelve oak trees are a tidy size and were one of my favourite haunts as a child. Today there are only eleven.

I know every inch of every field in Thingwall and surrounding villages. I walk the footpaths and lanes regularly. Although I have worked and travelled in many countries in Europe, Africa and the Far East, I still enjoy the local scenery and never tire of visiting the local beauty spots.

THE THREE BROOKS OF THINGWALL

There are three brooks in Thingwall : Landican Brook, Dale End Brook and Thingwall Brook.

Landican Brook drains the area around Thingwall Corner.

It is piped under Pensby Road, the round-a-bout and then under the first marl field, were the footpath stile is, before coming out of a land drain in the second field behind thick blackthorn bushes.

This brook was piped under Barnston Road well before living memory when road improvements were carried out. It is the Thingwall / Landican boundary for its entire length and flows into Prenton Brook at the mouth of Okells dell.

Dale End Brook started as a ditch years ago before all the housing development, at the side of the Emmanuel Church opposite *the Pensby Hotel* and ran past where Rylands Park is now built.

Today the ditch starts at the top of the field by Gwendoline Close. It runs past the bottom of Thorncroft Drive and picks up more water after flowing out of *Wacko's Pits* near the reservoir. After being piped under Barnston Road at Dale End it runs through the dales and joins Prenton Brook at the bridge in the bottom of the dale.

Like Landican Brook, Dale End Brook is an ancient boundary brook and is the Thingwall / Barnston boundary for its entire length.

Thingwall Brook is the only brook entirely in Thingwall itself and does not form a township boundary. It starts off somewhere between Seven Acres Lane and Axeholm Road, under the surface.

Years ago, the brook could be seen to start as a ditch in a field called *Sandy Hey* now under Regents Close. It carried on through another field called *Stony Wall*, now under the new houses on Sparks Lane. The water makes its way with the natural lay of the lands down the ancient ditch separating the bungalow *Wayside* and the cottage *Sandhay*, from the modern houses in Sparks Lane, built on a field called The Ditch.

Thingwall Brook, still a ditch, is piped under the Recreation Centre drive. Years ago, it ran down a *slack* at the side of the Recreation Centre. The *slack* was filled with rubble and levelled. The brook eventually gets piped under the Barnston Road. At last, it sees daylight alongside The *Basset Hound* at the bottom of a field called *Rye Hay*, sloping down from Cross Hill.

Thingwall Brook is now a proper brook and is piped once again, this time under Lower Thingwall Lane. Running through what are now the horse fields, it joins Landican Brook at *Gorsey Hill*.

All three brooks in Thingwall run water into *Prenton Brook*.

As *Prenton Brook* flows through Landican, close to the railway bridge where the Landican to Storeton lane is, it is joined by another brook. This brook, known locally as *The Gowy*, flows from under Station Road, Storeton, through Stanley Wood and under the railway via the 'Poachers Culvert' to join Prenton Brook. Stanley Wood was known locally as Landican Wood, although it is a few yards over the border and is in fact in Storeton.

There are two ancient wells in Stanley Wood and when I was a lad, I remember a cow falling down one. There must have been a few cottages there years ago as I can't see people digging one well, let alone two, so far from the nearest village.

Half a mile after *The Gowy*, a brook running out of Prenton Dell joins Prenton Brook. After this, Prenton Brook becomes the *River Fender*. Fender means 'slow flowing brook'. *The Fender* eventually joins the River Birket and flows into Birkenhead Docks and the Mersey.

FIELD NAMES

Field names tell us a lot about what the land was once like in Thingwall and the rest of Wirral. There are many Thingwall field names with heath, pit and marl in them, such as *Old Heath Field, Gala Pits* and *Marled Hay*. This tells us there was a lot of heathland and also clay and marl pits.

Vetch Field in Irby, *Horse Pasture* in Irby and Landican, *Rye Hay* in Thingwall and Irby, *Oxhay* in Pensby and *Long Cow Pasture* in Moreton are just a few of the Wirral field names which tell us what the fields were used for.

Hay or hey, is Anglo-Saxon meaning – enclosed land, usually near a house.

Backside and *Intake* are common field names all over Wirral, including Thingwall. *Backside* describes a field behind the farm and an *Intake* is a field claimed from common or waste land.

Fields called *Bleak Looms*, found in Thingwall (part of which Nurse Road is built on), and in Moreton, mean bleak land, from the Anglo Saxon word loon, meaning land. *Lower Out Gates*, which the older property in Barnsdale Avenue is built on, means out lying pastures near a right of way.

Field names with the word *Glebe* in them, such as *Glebe Hey*, now under the Woodchurch Estate, belonged to the Parish Church. Glebe comes from the Latin – Gleba – meaning clod. In the 1840s, Heswall Parish had 20 acres of glebe land, Woodchurch 50 acres and West Kirby 66 acres.

There are many Wirral field names with the words *Carr*, *Hooks*, *Holme* and *Pingle* in them, such as *Saughall Carr*, *Moreton Hooks*, *Holme Hay* and *The Pingle*, (often spelt *Pringle*).

Carr is old English meaning marsh and a *Hook* is a field jutting out into a waterway or marsh. A *Pingle* is a field surrounded by deep ditches and *Holme* is Norse for river or marsh island. In later years it came to describe a water meadow.

Holme is also an Old English name for a holly bush.

Many of these field names are found in low lying areas, particularly in Moreton, Leasowe, Bidston and the Carr Lane area between Meols and Hoylake which are still marshy and were always prone to tidal flooding.

In Landican Township, there is a *Hooks* field and a *Carr Bridge Meadow* now a rugby pitch by the Woodchurch flyover.

There must have been an old bridge across the marsh and *River Fender*, where the ancient footpath to Oxton is. Hence the field name.

A *Pike* is a field, which runs to a point, and a small field usually adjoining a house or farm is called a *croft*.

Field names with *hungry* in it such as *Hungry Oxton* in Upton, usually describe a field which takes a lot of fertilizer to give a good crop.

The Vikings left their mark in many different field names as well as village names.

In Bidston Township, there are field names with the Norse word *Thwaite* in them, which means – clearing.

In Irby Village, the lane alongside *Yew Tree Farm*, leads to an ancient pasture field behind Arrowe Brook Motors, several acres of which were farmed in the last century, by Irish born farmer, John McCave of *Caves Farm*.

In this field, the ancient ridges and deep furrows between them from the Saxon days of strip farming, can clearly be seen, especially on the sloping section running up to the new bungalows.

This field is called *Heskeths*, which is Norse meaning – horse race field – and was obviously the venue for Viking sporting events. It's not a bad mushroom field some years either.

Some fields have more colourful names such as *Hare and Hounds* field down Gills Lane, which runs alongside *Marl Field Lane*. *Coney Graves* in Heswall doesn't sound as if it was a healthy field for the local rabbit population.

Many field names seem impossible to explain accurately, such as *Two Loves* and *Big Two Loaves* close to Thingwall Reservoir and *Whelpers* near Lower Thingwall Lane. Also, *Swans* down Gallopers Lane, *Shocking Dale* behind the B.U.P.A. Hospital, and *Dig Meat* in Landican.

Hundreds of Wirral field names must have been lost over the years. I have a family will dated 1807 which names 27 Moreton fields. On the tithe map and apportionments 31 years later, 13 fields of the 27 fields mentioned, do not exist. Possibly two or three small crofts have been made into one large field, taking the name of the biggest croft.

One of the farms mentioned in the will is *Ley House. Ley* comes from the Anglo-Saxon, *Leah*, a meadow.

There are also a tremendous number of Wirral fields named after their past owners or tenants. Examples are *Youngs Intake* named after an Irby Yoeman and *Breretons Meadow,* named after William de Brereton of Moreton.

LANE AND ROAD NAMES

Just as field names do, lane and road names tell us a lot about our local history. Some were named after people who lived in the area, fields they were built on, or buildings they led to.

Roads on the Woodchurch Estate are nearly all named after the fields they were built on. Some other examples are Antons Road, Porto Hey Road and Far Meadow in Irby. In the Heswall area Whitfield Lane, Napps Way, Wittering Lane and in Moreton, Sandbrook Lane, to name just a few.

All over Wirral there are School, Mill, Market, Grange and Lime Kiln lanes, streets and roads which tell us where they once led, or still lead to. Grange was land belonging to the Monks.

Quite a few local highways were named after people who lived in or near them. Some examples are, farmer Jack Sparks of Thingwall, Whaley's (Yeomen of Pensby and Irby), Gills of Barnston, Downhams of Heswall and Newburns and Williams of Oxton.

Some Wirral roads were named by prominent people who built them, for example, Lord Vyner of Bidston, Lord Leverhulme, builder of Levers Causeway, John Laird of Birkenhead and his mother, who's maiden name 'Hamilton', he gave to the square.

In Irby, local builder, John 'Cornelius' Devaney built Cornelius Drive and Brian Avenue, named after his son.

Some old Wirral lane names have changed over the years due to miss spelling. Examples are Salacre Lane, Upton, Danger Lane in Moreton and Limbo Lane on the border of Arrowe and Irby.

Salacre Lane was originally a dead end, called Sally Carr Lane, owing to the boggy land it ran through. From *sealh* a willow and *carr* a marsh. Danghs, is an old word for black shale, which probably floored Danger Lane.

Limbo Lane, off Thingwall Road, was access to two Irby fields called *Little Limbers* and *Big Limbers*. It was originally called Limbers Lane. This can clearly be seen on the 1846 tithe map of Arrowe Township.

Natural features such as brooks and hills obviously gave their names to local highways. For instance, Arrowe Brook Road, Holt Hill in Tranmere, and Pool Lane, Woodchurch. Holt is Anglo-Saxon meaning a wood.

Pool Lane took it's name from a large public drinking pit or pool filled in before the Woodchurch Estate was built. Years ago travellers watered their horses there and thrashing machine gangs drew water from the pit for their steam engines.

One lane with an unusual name was Mad Dog Lane, on the 1838 Moreton tithe map. John Spurious was killed by a mad dog in Moreton in 1748. The lane was probably the scene of the tragedy.

THE FARMING COMMUNITY OF LANDICAN

Thingwall is a small town and no longer a village, yet Landican which has always had close ties with Thingwall, has hardly changed since the last century and before.

In 1851 the only township bordering Thingwall with a smaller population than Landican, was Pensby. Landican consisted of nine houses occupied by 51 people. Pensby had five houses with 41 inhabitants.

The road names were different in the 1800s. Woodchurch Road was called Ferry Road and in the 1880s it was changed to Prenton Road. Arrowe Park Road was called Chester Road and then Thingwall Road in the 1890s.

Landican, like Thingwall, was a well watered village. There were two wells and two springs.

One well is covered in Okells Farm and the other was half way down the old Woodchurch Lane, behind the cemetery in what was once a cottage garden.

One spring was near to the footpath from Thingwall, just before Okells Farm and the other was at the side of Landican Lane, just before its junction with Woodchurch Road. This stretch of lane was diverted about 1969 as it ran into the newly constructed motorway slip road by the pumping station. Landican Lane now comes out onto Woodchurch Road, opposite the car park, next to the Pioneer supermarket.

Until 1934, access to Landican, by road from Thingwall, was gained via Arrowe Park Road and Woodchurch Lane. Woodchurch Lane was an ancient highway, which was part of a network of bridle paths and lanes used by priests travelling between Woodchurch Church and St. Andrews Church in Bebington. It started on Woodchurch Road, close to what is now Arrowe Park roundabout and ran behind Landican cemetery, joining Landican Lane at Landican Village.

In 1934 the 'new' Landican Road was built by Warrens, from Thingwall Corner to Landican Village and Woodchurch Lane was closed to traffic. The middle section of Woodchurch Lane was incorporated in the cemetery and planted with trees. It remained open only as a very muddy public footpath until 1944 when it was closed by Act of Parliament, but access to the cottages was still available.

When travelling from Thingwall Corner to Landican, the old Woodchurch Lane, (now a farm track), can be seen on the left at the first bend, blocked off by a black steel gate. The other end of the lane, close to Arrowe Park bus stop, is now access to allotments.

In 1930 there were 13 dwellings within the boundary of Landican. All were either farms or farm workers tied cottages. Seven are still standing. One is a brick house facing Arrowe Park roundabout and backing onto the cemetery allotments. Four are in the village itself, *Old Hall Farm*, *Home Farm*, *The Poplars* and *Farm View*. The other two are semi-detached cottages, numbers 1 and 2 Landican Lane, near the Woodchurch Road end.

The other six have been demolished. Two stood where the Pioneer supermarket is built, one was opposite Thingwall Corner, two were halfway along the old Woodchurch Lane and the other was at the mouth of the old lane, behind the present bus shelter.

THE THREE FARMS

In the 1880s, Peter Okell, of *Old Hall Farm* rented 162 acres, Mrs. Ziegler of *Home Farm* 285, acres and in 1850 Mrs. Broster of *The Poplars* 174 acres. In those days the whole of Landican was owned by John Wilson Patten. In later years the township was owned by the Hon. Lady Lumley, who sold it to the present owner, Lord Leverhulme.

Old Hall Farm has been in the Okell family for four generations. They moved in when Scotsman, Mr. Dalzell, left in the 1870s. When my Grandad was young, Peter Okell was tenant. Peter was born in Little Leigh in 1828 and lived in Shipbrook in Cheshire when he was first married, before coming to Landican. In my Dad's younger days, Peter's son, Ralph, ran the farm, then after him, his son, Kirk,(who was about my Dad's age). Today Kirk's son, Peter, is the tenant of *Old Hall Farm*.

Home Farm, across the lane, has changed hands many times. When my Grandad was young, Mrs. Mary Ziegler, who was born in Liverpool in 1828, was tenant. Then when my Dad was a lad, at the time of the Great War, Cuthbert Becket rented *Home Farm*. He passed the tenancy on to one of his relations, Mr. Caine, who went bankrupt. Then, from the late 1920s, Ralph Leech was tenant, until 1936 and when he moved to a farm in Raby and his son Ralph, took the tenancy of *Storeton Hall Farm*, Mr. J. Alexander Duncan, the present farmer moved in to *Home Farm*.

Home Farm, Landican, one of the largest local farms.

Mr. Duncan was a fine rugby player when he was young and years ago, he was also a magistrate. Alf Oxton, whose father, Joe, rented *The Warrens*, has worked for Mr. Duncan since 1947. In the past, Alf has lived in number 2 and number 3 Landican Lane, but he has lived in his fathers old house in Pensby Road, Thingwall for many years. Alf is a very interesting person to talk to and he is a well-liked member of the local community.

During the middle of the last century the Broster family were tenants of *The Poplars* and eventually in about 1890 the Turton family came from Raby. Edwin Turton left Landican in the late 1920s to manage his Mothers farm in Halewood. Edwin's South African brother in law, James Hinde, who was also his farm bailiff, became the next tenant of *The Poplars*.

Half the land belonging to *The Poplars*, was taken over by Birkenhead Corporation when the 88 acre Landican Cemetery was built in 1934 and Mr. Hinde retired. *The Poplars* ceased to be a working farm and the remainder of the land was divided between *Home Farm* and *Old Hall Farm*.

Today *The Poplars* is the home of Mr. Michael Groves. Michael is a grain merchant and in his acre of gardens and orchard he keeps a few poultry and a couple of sheep as a hobby. In his younger days he was a first class cricketer and played for Oxford University and Somerset.

TIED COTTAGES.

Tied cottages changed hands often years ago. When a farmworker died or went to work elsewhere, the cottage had to be vacated. From the 1930s things became more civilised and the strict rules were not always applied.

Old Dave Prince, (who worked as a stone quarryman most of his life), moved from Barnston to live in one of two cottages on Woodchurch Road where the Pioneer supermarket is built. Although these cottages were in Landican township (as is part of the Woodchurch Estate) they were tied to *Home Farm*, Woodchurch.

Alf Lyons and Dave Prince's son, young Dave, lived in numbers 1 and 2 Landican Lane, which were tied to *Home Farm*, Landican. Today, Alfs widow lives in number one.

Dave left *Home Farm*, rented at the time by Ralph Leech, and went to work as cowman across the road, for Ralph Okell. He had to get out of the tied cottage and moved next door to the Francom's in Holmwood Drive, Thingwall. Dave's son Bill also worked at Okells. My Dad says Dave was a first class farm worker and could tackle any task.

Okells used to keep sheep in those days and Dave Prince used to do all the shearing.

The two reasonably modern cottages, numbers 3 and 4 halfway down Landican Lane, were built in 1936.

In the 1920's and 1930s, Bill Candeland and Joey Hewson lived in the two old semi detached cottages, behind the cemetery in Woodchurch Lane.

My Dad used to pick up peelings from them for his pigs. Joey Hewson worked on *Home Farm* and Bill Candeland worked on *Old Hall Farm*. The Candelands originally came from the Shotwick area and one or two lived in Neston.

After Bill Candeland moved out, Mr. and Mrs. Freddy Bowden moved into the cottage in the 1940s.

One night a pup belonging to Mrs. Bowden got out. In the middle of the night she could hear whimpering coming from the cemetery. She put her coat on and went looking for it and found the pup had fallen down a freshly dug grave. There was a short gravedigger's ladder near by and she climbed down it and rescued the pup. Not a thing many women would chance doing.

Edgar Brown, one of 'Foxy' Browns grandsons, lived in the other half of the cottage after Joey Hewson. Both Freddy and Edgar worked on George Bowden's farm.

After Freddy died in the early 1950s aged 82, the cottages were pulled down and Mrs. Bowden was given a new house on the Woodchurch Estate.

At the end of the old Woodchurch Lane, behind the present 'bus stop, close to Arrowe Park roundabout was another old farmers tied cottage. It was home to the Duckers family in 1920's and in later years to another family of farm workers, the Chadwicks. The Chadwicks were a big family and many of them worked on Okells farm at one time or another. Septimus, (so christened because he was the seventh son), was cowman at Okells for many years. Their cottage was demolished at the same time as Freddy Bowdens.

In Landican village, the white house, *Farm View*, used to be the home of the farm bailiff of *Home Farm* opposite.

In the early years of this century, Sam Wilbraham, my Uncle Chuck's Dad, was bailiff at *Home Farm* for Mr. Becket. Sam was born in Storeton and worked on local farms nearly all his life. After he left, Scotsman Bob Paisley became bailiff and moved into *Farm View*.
His son was a carpenter and repaired all the farm gates, buildings, carts, etc., in the village and also made wheel barrows.

Landican Lane A quiet corner of Wirral.
Left: *Farm View*, years ago the home of the farm bailiffs of *Home Farm*.
Right: *The Poplars* once a working farm.

David Evans from Shropshire, worked as teamsman at *The Poplars*, for Edwin Turton, after moving from Raby to Landican in the 1890s. He lived in the tied brick cottage opposite Arrowe Park roundabout. Davé died in 1908 aged only 42. His son David got a job as a gardener at *Arrowe Hall* and lived in a bothy on the estate.

Mr. Chorley took over as teamsman and moved into the cottage. His son Charley followed in his footsteps and worked all his life on Landican farms. Until a few years ago I used to see him early in the morning, walking to *Home Farm* for his can of milk. He is a very old man now and has moved from his cottage, number 2 Landican Lane, to sheltered accommodation in Heswall.

At Thingwall Corner, opposite the roundabout, where Landican Road now begins, once stood *Pear Tree Cottage* built about 1860 at 191 feet above sea level. From 1891 until the 1920s, it was the home of William Egerton, born in Loppington, Shropshire in 1854. William was Turtons other teamsman. He moved into the tied cottage from Woodchurch with his wife Emma who was a laundress.

In the 1920s Bill had a counter at his cottage and sold sweets, pop and cigarettes to ramblers and locals. The Egerton family moved to *Ninga* up the Pensby Road. Tommy Croker the jockey married Lol Leay and they eventually moved in. In the early 1930's Thingwall Corner was widened and *Pear Tree Cottage* was pulled down. The big old garden pear tree, which gave the cottage its name, is still standing, on the green opposite Thingwall Corner roundabout, in front of the sub station.

Home Farm and *Old Hall Farm* are still big farms. Their fields are separated by Landican Lane and the Landican to Storeton Lane, up to the railway bridge by Stanley Wood. The Landican and Thingwall farms have pretty well been worked and rented by Wirral or Lancashire families.

However, in the last century, Arrowe had a high proportion of Irish and Scottish immigrants. Several farm tenants were Scottish, such as the MacFarlanes of *Top House Farm* and the Morrisons of *Arrowe House Farm* and practically all the farm labourers were Irish.

The large number of Irish immigrants in Wirral was understandable so soon after the potato famine. In 1851 in Liverpool, out of a population of 375,843 there were 83,813 Irish born. Chester had 2,032 Irish born and every town and village in Wirral had its share of immigrants.

Arrowe and Landican still have considerable farm land and open spaces. Thingwall has suffered by far the most from the 20th century.

In Saxon and Norman times, Landican was far bigger and more populous than Thingwall. How things have changed – Landican is still a country hamlet, yet so close to the town. Thingwall is more or less a small town.

Looking down Landican Lane from *Farm View Farm* 1992

The Poplars, Landican Lane

WOODCHURCH

Woodchurch was once part of Landican. The ancient church dates back to Saxon times.

It was probably called Woodchurch because it was originally constructed of wood, or because it was built in a wood. (From the Anglo-Saxon *Wudu* – a wood.)

In the Middle Ages it was compulsory for all able bodied men to practice with bow and arrows. The church, being the centre of the community, was where the archers met and Woodchurch was no exception. The parish provided archers for the Welsh and French wars.

Yew trees provided the best bows, but because their leaves are poisonous, they were planted in walled churchyards out of reach of livestock.

Entrance to Woodchurch churchyard is gained through the old *lych* gate. These old covered gateways were built for mourners to shelter under while awaiting the priest. Lych is old English for corpse. Years ago it was considered bad luck to be the first mourner through the gate or for a bride and groom to enter the church through it.

In the 13th century, Woodchurch Church was called St. Peter's, but for hundreds of years it has been the Holy Cross.

It has been my family's parish church for about 350 years. One of my ancestors, Nathaniel Dawson, Yeoman of Irby, was Churchwarden in 1736.

When entering the churchyard through the lych gate, the path is found to be about six foot below the level of the old grave stones, such as those of my family on the right. This is because over the centuries soil has been continually brought to the top and replaced by corpses. Thus high banks are built up.

The old Parish of Woodchurch consisted of nine townships and part of three others in the 1700's. They were Woodchurch, Landican, Thingwall, Pensby, Barnston, Arrowe, Prenton, Oxton, Noctorum and part of Irby, Upton and Claughton. These townships totalled 5,792 acres including 50 acres of glebe land.

In 1724 there were only twelve births, seven marriages and twenty five deaths in the whole parish. Obviously 1724 was a bad year for sickness.

The population of the parish was very small, but in the middle of the last century it began to grow rapidly.

In 1841 the village of Woodchurch consisted of 19 houses with 114 inhabitants. By 1851 the population of the village had fallen slightly to 110, but the parish as a whole had grown considerably to 2,927. There were 1,384 males and 1,543 females living in 547 houses. Oxton was by far the biggest township in the parish, with 389 houses and 2,007 inhabitants, mainly due to its close proximity to Birkenhead.

In the middle of the last century, the main landowners in Woodchurch were, John Wilson Patten and the Reverend Joshua King, who was a crack shot and employed his own gamekeeper.

There were several minor landowners, among them the Inglefields, who were quite an important family. They owned Lee's smithy, the *Horse and Jockey*, a wheelwright's shop and a few acres of farmland. They were close friends of the Cappers of *Thingwall Mill*.

There was another pub, in Church Terrace, *The Ring 'O' Bells*, managed by John Gertrey.

Just how poor local people were in the last century is illustrated in the school logbook, by the attendance records of 1873. Occasional poor attendance was due to parents sending their children mushrooming, blackberrying, working in the fields and beating game on shoots at *Arrowe Hall*.

It was a mixed school. Lessons commenced at 7.00 am in the summer and at 8.00 am in the winter, with an average attendance of 107 in the 1890s. In those days the principal landowner in Woodchurch was the Hon. Mrs. Lumley.

CHARITIES

A lot of money has been left to Woodchurch Parish over the years. There were two cow charities in the parish. In 1525, John Goodacre left twenty marks which was used to buy 39 cows. The poor could then rent them out, at 2 shillings and 8 pence (13½p) a year.

Richard Sherlock, born in Oxton, gave money to start a cow charity in his native village. He graduated M.A. in Dublin in 1633 and was chaplain to one of Charles Stuart's Cavalier Regiments in the Civil War. In 1670, Richard gave £50 to the Woodchurch bread charity and in 1677 he gave another £50 to buy fifteen cows for rental by the poor of Oxton at 2 shillings and 6 pence (12½p) a year.

In 1665 William Gleave founded the Parish School. He gave £400 to build the school and £100 to build a School House. Thomas Gleave, born in Burton, left £50 in 1670 to be invested in land and the interest spent on bread to be given to the poor on Sundays. He also left money to five other Wirral Parishes.

Both cow charities were still going in my Grandad's youth. Then Oxton was down to 11 cows and bread was given out to the poor on Sundays, by Reverend Robin.

THE ROBIN FAMILY

In 1861 the Curate of Woodchurch, Philip Robin, became Rector upon the death of his uncle, Joshua King. The Reverend Philip Robin was responsible for sixty three acres of glebe and park land and also managed the cow charity. In 1874, he buried my Great, Great Grandfather. In 1897 he passed away himself and was succeeded by his son, Reverend Percival Robin.

By the early years of this century, the cow charity had become obsolete. However, Reverend Percival Robin, farmed fields round Pool Lane and kept three or four cows. Even in the 1920's he gave free milk to any family in the village with a new baby.

Reverend Percival Robin buried my Great Grandfather in 1911. He retired, aged 75 in 1931 and passed away at Fron Huelog, Bettws-y-Coed in 1932.

Bryan Robin became Reverend of Woodchurch upon his father's retirement in 1931. In 1932, he married my mother and father. Reverend Bryan Robin became Canon of Chester in 1940 and in 1941 was consecrated Bishop of Adelaide, Australia, by the Archbishop of Canterbury.

The Robin's are buried at Woodchurch.

HOME FARM, WOODCHURCH

The Woodchurch Estate is built on *Home Farm*. In the 1890s it was farmed by George Ziegler who also farmed *Home Farm*, Landican. In the early years of this century, Samuel Croxton became tenant. During the Great War it was farmed by George 'Widger' Waring and then the Royden family. Ernest Royden also had a small farm called *Bridge Hay*, which stood on the Woodchurch side of Ford Road, half way between Upton Village and Upton Station. Altogether they had a big acreage and employed three farm bailiffs.

There was crime even in those more law-abiding days. One bailiff was robbed in Upton, after drawing the farm wages from the post office.

In the late 1920s, Mr. Ball left *Oaklands Farm* in Heswall and took over *Home Farm* from the Roydens. He brought farm bailiff Mr. Freddy Bowden and family with him to run the farm.

The farmland on the higher ground was good land and the annual rent was £1 an acre in the 1920s. Down below, near the *River Fender*, (now the Carr Bridge Road area), was very marshy and the rent was only 10 shillings (50p) an acre.

Liverpool hay dealers, Sturgeon's, used to buy loads of hay from Mr. Ball, and other farmers in the area. Old Ned Goldburn of Tranmere, used to do a bit of hay trussing in the Woodchurch and Landican areas, but Sturgeons usually brought their own trusser, Jim Berry, from Aintree. After a price had been agreed for the stack, Jim would truss the hay and load the carts. He had to keep the loads down a layer or two, owing to Prenton Railway Bridge.

Sturgeon's horses were not used to marshy ground and had difficulty getting loaded carts off the *Carr* fields. George Bowden used his team to get the carts to the road. One cart horse George had, called Duke, used to rear up and dig his hind hooves in, then lower his weight down onto the collar and push at the same time. They reckoned he could free any cart.

Being a large farm, a lot of casual Irish labour was used at harvest time. Many of the men could neither read nor write. On paydays, Mrs. Bowden used to write to all their families and send 10 shillings (50p) of their wages home, lest they boozed all their pay.

One family, which worked for Freddy Bowden, came over from Ireland for generations. They were the Prendergasts, from Castlebar, in County Mayo. Thomas Prendergast was a real grafter, he and his sons, John and Martin, all worked for the Bowdens.

They are descendants of the Norman Knight, Maurice de Prendergast or one of his followers, who went to Ireland, from Prendergast in South Wales.

In 1926, Martin went to work on the tunnel gang, digging the Mersey road tunnel. He was injured in a rock fall, breaking a leg, but luckily he survived. Martin's daughter, Mrs. Mary Davies, is District Manageress for Sayers Confectioners and lives in Gwendoline Close, Thingwall, and his son, Danny, is a self-employed steel erector from Bebington.

The Prendergasts were renowned for their hard work.

In 1933, Mr. Ball died and the Bowden family left Woodchurch and went their separate ways.

George and his wife Molly lived next door to my Aunt Jane in Pensby for a while, then when my Dad left *The Piggery*, in Thingwall, George became the new tenant. His Dad, Freddy, moved into the old cottage in Woodchurch Lane and worked on John Milner's farm in Barnston. When George got on his feet, his Dad went to work for him.

Ralph Leech of *Home Farm*, Landican also took the tenancy of *Home Farm*, Woodchurch when Mr. Ball died, until about 1940 when Welshman Wilf Roberts became the last farmer at *Home Farm*, Woodchurch.

ARROW PARK GATES.

Arrowe Park Gates.
The *Horse and Jockey* inn and Lees smithy (in the centre of the picture),
have long since been replaced by the *Arrowe Park Hotel* and car parks.

SOME WOODCHURCH FAMILIES OF THE 1920s

Just like any other village in the 1920's, there were people who came and went, and families who stayed for some time.

The Lee family was originally from West Kirby. They were blacksmiths and mechanical engineers and worked the foundry in Woodchurch for about 100 years.

In the 1870's they also ran *Yew Tree Farm* in Irby. My Dad knew the Lee's well, their busy foundry was where the Arrowe Park pub back carpark is today. Another Woodchurch blacksmith was Frank Morris.

In the early years of this century, Mrs. Elizabeth Johnson and then the Duckers family were tenants of the *Horse and Jockey*, but before the Great War Septimus Broster took over and ran the pub into the 1920s.

The Underwood and Minnie families walked to Woodchurch from Northampton in the 1890's, for work on the construction of the Bidston to Chester railway line. Mrs. Underwood and Mrs. Minnie were sisters. Jim Minnie lived in a white cottage down School Lane. He eventually became foreman of the Upton to Heswall stretch of the line. Every Sunday morning he had the task of walking the line with a hammer to test the wedges.

Jim and Mr. Underwood were keen rabbiters, and on Sunday mornings combined business with pleasure by taking their two whippets along the line with them. A few busy bodies complained to Jim's boss about the dogs nailing rabbits here and there, and they finished up selling them.

The Underwoods lived next door to the Ducker's family, in a cottage, which once stood, where the flats are, roughly opposite Arrowe Park Hospital. Mr. Underwood's daughter, Edith, married Frank Bowden, from *Home Farm*. Frank was a farm worker and then a 'bus driver for the Crosville, and lived most of his life down Gills Lane. His son, Frank, also a former farm worker, lives in Whaley Lane, Irby.

Joe Johnson, a keen pigeon fancier, lived in a cottage a bit higher up the main road from the Underwoods, towards Pool Lane. He was the local wheelwright and joiner.

For many years the Randles family lived in one of three houses, called *Woodchurch Yard*. Jack Randles was horseman for my Dad at *Ivy Farm*, Moreton, for a while in the late 1930s.

One day, Dad asked Jack Randles and George Saxon to go down to Leasowe Fields and draw out a few ridges with the horse and plough. When they arrived there, they found they had forgotten the marker pegs. George said, "Never mind, Jack, I'll stand at the other end of the field and you aim the plough for me". Jack made a start. Three or four times he stopped the horses to adjust the plough and set the depth of the ridge. Each time he stopped, George sidestepped a yard or two. When Jack reached the other end of the field, George asked him, "Are you having bother with your eyes?" "Not yet", replied Jack. "Well then, asked George, how did you plough a ridge like a banana?"

Jack looked round at the bent ridge, then turned back to see George rolling in the grass laughing his cap off. Daft I suppose, but it's the daft things that amuse a lot of us. Jack and George laughed about that for years.

Jack suffered a lot with his chest and Dad used to bike it up to Woodchurch in the 1930's to see him when he was bad in bed. He never recovered enough to be ploughman again.

Dave Evans, Turton's teamsman's son, was one of 16 *Arrowe Hall* gardeners under Mr. McFee. In 1914 he married my aunt Jane. It was a double wedding ceremony along with my Dad's other sister, Aunt Lizzie, who wed Uncle Chuck Wilbraham, the chauffeur for Stern's.
Aunt Jane and Uncle Dave lived in *Church Terrace*, owned by the Rev. Robin.

When they moved out to live in the 1¾ acre Pensby market garden, Laurel Cottage, now under the Gulf Garage, Aunt Polly and Uncle Ron Kitchenman moved in from a caravan in Thingwall. Uncle Ron got a boss's job on the Water Board and they eventually moved to Tower Road, Heswall. Their only son, Cousin Jimmy, was a very good footballer. He was killed on a motorbike, it broke their hearts.

My three cousins, Geoff, Dennis and Frank Evans are sons of which Aunt Jane can be proud.

Geoff started work as a 'bus conductor for Crosville, at Heswall 'Bus Station, in 1933. In those days the Heswall 'buses had no numbers, just the destinations. When the war started he joined up and served a full six years in the army.

When he was de-mobbed, he returned to Crosville and became a driver. By this time the 'buses had numbers. The Heswall to Birkenhead, via Pensby, was number 114. From the 1950's, it was the F.19. In 1965, Geoff was promoted to inspector and worked his way up to Chief Inspector before retiring in 1980 after 47 years and 7 months service.

He brought his family up in the sandstone house next door but one to The *8 O'Clock Shop* on Pensby Road before moving to his present home in Parkgate. His son, John, kept one of the family traditions going and went to sea. He was a Radio Officer for many years for the Blue Funnel Line, the same company I sailed with a few times.

Dennis Evans served in the Royal Marines during the war and was captured in Crete. When he was released he worked as a joiner at Lairds. Dennis also lives in Parkgate.

His son, Peter Dawson Evans, a Neston joiner, has kept another family tradition alive. That of woodworking, which began over 200 years ago with John Dawson, a Moreton cooper, who was buried in Woodchurch in 1788.

Frank Evans followed our other family occupation and for years worked on Totty's farm, in Heswall bottom village and then for Heswall Council. Frank has lived in Irby Road for many years.

Clive, one of his sons was a professional footballer and played for Tranmere, Wigan and Stockport County. Nowadays, he plays in the Birkenhead Sunday League first division for Irby, with my eldest son, Greg.

Another family living in *Church Terrace* in the 1920's was that of George Phillips. George was born in Irby in 1875 and moved to Thingwall in the 1880's when his young widowed Mother married farm worker, Thomas Williams. He served his time as an apprentice gardener in the 1890's. George was sexton of Woodchurch Church and parish clerk in the 1920's. He also went round the farms with a big stallion, for which people paid him to line their mares, a sideline, which George Merrit, of Oxton brickworks also had.

There was not a lot of full time employment in Wirral during the 1920's and 1930s and many young men emigrated. George Phillips' son Albert, Haja Bowden of *Home Farm* and Tony Lyons of Landican, all went to Canada for work.

In those days, would be employers met the boats and picked out who they wanted. Albert got a job in a sawmill and Haja and Tony were offered farm work.

Haja finished up on a farm out in the wilderness working for a Russian, eating nothing but salt pork, still with hair on.

Eventually, the three lads came back to Wirral. Just before they left, Albert Phillips cut his thumb badly in the sawmill. During the homeward voyage the cut turned bad. By the time he got home, gangrene had set in and he died.

Albert's brother, Ted, was a verger at Woodchurch Church. In later years he moved to *Greenhays Cottages* in Barnston and worked as a maintenance man at Thingwall Reservoir. Ted's son, Rod, is an old mate of mine and today lives at *Greenhays* with his wife and family.

Church Terrace, once part of the old country village of Woodchurch.

There were two families of Bennets in *Church Terrace*. Annie Bennett and her mother lived on the corner and Mr. and Mrs. Tom Bennett and their son Vin, who worked on the Crosville buses, lived in another cottage.

The Mutch family had a shop in Woodchurch village for donkey's years. George Mutch ran the shop and also worked as a gardener for Reverend Robin. George's son, Young George, worked on the Crosville and his other son, Sam, was second horseman at Okells Farm, Landican.

Sam Mutch, Ralph Leech of *Home Farm*, Landican, and my Dad, knocked about together and often used to go to dances in Birkenhead.

Sam met a young schoolmistress at one of the dances. A few years later they married and they took the tenancy of a farm of their own in Barnston.

Woodchurch was a lovely village years ago, even in the 1950's when I was a lad. I remember the old sandstone cottages standing derelict in 1960 waiting to be pulled down.

Another little community gone.

Woodchurch is a small town now. Only the road names and its ancient church remind us of it's rural past.

The Horse and Jockey. (Demolished 1937. The newly built Arrowe Park Hotel is to the rear)

Lee's Smithy. (Now the Arrowe Park Hotel car park)

WIRRAL CASTLES

Many people have asked me if there were any castles in Wirral. As far as I know, the only castle in Wirral was *Shotwick Castle*. It was built by the Normans during the reign of William II, to protect the ford across the River Dee from Welsh raids into Cheshire.

In those days, the castle was only a furlong from the river. Now it is miles away, because the course of the Dee was altered and the Wirral coast has silted up. A few miles of Wales are now on the Wirral side of the Dee.

Shotwick Castle was reputed to have a five-storey watchtower. Now all that remains is a grassy mound, on private land.

Leasowe Castle, built in the 16th century by the Earls of Derby, was never a true castle – more a secure grand house.

It was not referred to as a castle until after 1800. Before that it was called *Mockbeggar Hall*.

There were a number of fortified manor houses in Wirral. Among them are *Greasby Old Hall*, *Puddington Old Hall*, *Brimstage Hall*, *Irby Hall*, *Gayton Hall* and *Farr Hall*, which once stood in Heswall.

Puddington Old Hall was once the seat of a branch of the powerful Massey family who fought in the Welsh and French wars. Sir John Massey of Puddington, lieutenant of North Wales, was killed in 1403 at the battle of Shrewsbury.

This medieval manor house was once protected by a moat and drawbridge. The ancient dovecot still survives.

The building of Brimstage Hall was probably started in the 14th century by the 'Domvilles'. They held Oxton, Raby, Barnston and Thingwall. This strong tower house was protected by a moat, three sides of which can still be traced.

Irby Hall was built in the 17th century, on the fortified site of the ancient manor of the monks of St. Werburghs. The moat around the hall was almost certainly dug as protection against Welsh raids.

Looking over the wall from the roadside footpath, the stretch of moat to the left of the hall can clearly be seen.

There was a well in the grounds close to the wall and also a dovecot. Dovecots and wells were extremely important in a siege situation.

Doves and pigeons were a cheap reliable source of fresh meat. They could fly out and feed themselves in woods and fields, on crops, clover and acorns etc.

LOCAL WILDLIFE

My sons and I often walk the local fields and footpaths. A special interest of ours is watching wildlife, although there is not as much as there used to be.

Rabbits originally from Spain were brought to Wirral and the rest of England by the Normans who kept them in enclosures and bred them for meat. Some escaped and they gradually spread nationwide.

Although there are still a few rabbits about, their numbers and territory alter drastically with the periodic outbreak of myxomatosis.

Myxomatosis is a disease developed in Uruguay, which spread to Wirral and the rest of Britain via France in 1953.

A few hares, the odd pheasant and covey of partridge get up when the dogs are working. My whippet lurchers sometimes flush a woodcock or fox out of the ditches and you never know what else.

There are more stoats and weasels than you might expect, but we are only lucky enough to see them now and again.

Over the years I've come across a few reasonably unusual finds in Thingwall fields, such as a partridge nest with fifteen eggs in under a bush near the reservoir. Another morning, I found a hunting hawk hanging upside down from a barbed wire fence by its leather jesses, not far from Landican Brook. I've also seen a few unusual visitors to Thingwall fields, such as a buzzard being mobbed by crows at 5 o'clock one morning and also on a Saturday afternoon.

One winter's day, I saw a skein of six greylag geese come down to rest on *Gorsey Hill*, near Lower Thingwall Lane. This horse field has now been sold off in two acre strips at between five and seven thousand pounds an acre.

Badgers are not a common sight and I've only seen two in the fields of Thingwall, and not recently. There used to be a big sett in the Sanatorium grounds, but when the B.U.P.A. hospital was built, it was bulldozed over.

There are no otters in Wirral. The last two were killed in the River Birket, near Moreton, about 1850.

The only snake I've ever seen in Wirral came into our farm scullery in 1957. My mother thought it was rope and when she bent down to pick it up, it spat out its tongue. She screamed and Dad ran in and chopped its head off with a shovel.
In school the next day, we had nature study and I told my teacher all about the snake, how big it was, what it looked like and everything else. When I got home I rushed to tell Dad what the teacher had to say. I said "guess what Dad, the teacher reckons that snake was harmless". Dad replied "it is now owd'n."

Years ago, one sight I enjoyed now and again was the hunt of the Royal Rock Beagles.

The Royal Rock is the oldest pack of beagles in England and originated in Rock Ferry.

When I was a lad, they were kennelled in Ledsham. They hunted hares around Storeton every season and sometimes came across Landican and Thingwall fields.

When the M53 mid-Wirral motorway was built, it became too dangerous to hunt this area and another link with country life was lost.

With 'keepered' estates like *Arrowe Hall* a thing of the past, and places like B.U.P.A. Hospital grounds and Landican cemetery being 'no go' areas for farmers and game-keepers, it's small wonder that vermin are on the increase. Foxes, magpies, jays and squirrels flourish in these havens and they seem to be everywhere.

Foxes were seldom seen years ago. Today they are seen even in the town. With the introduction of wheelie bins, their main source of food has been cut off. Household pets will have to be more securely housed from now on.

Due to magpies and squirrels, birds like the thrush, which build a fairly obvious nest, have been decimated. The 'throstle', as it was called years ago, is not often seen on the lawn nowadays. The dunny is less common too.

With Thingwall fields being small and well hedged, they still hold a reasonable amount of bird life. Lately, I've been surprised at the number of goldfinches, long tailed tits and Jenny wrens about.

When we go for a walk, we look out for things such as mushrooms, hazelnuts and walkingsticks in the hedges, farm animals and anything to add interest to our walk.

I've taught my children to enjoy and respect our local countryside and I hope the open spaces of Thingwall and surrounding villages remain for them and their children to enjoy.

A WELL KNOWN LOCAL COUNTRYMAN

Alf Oxton milking at *Home Farm,* Landican during the 1960s

SOME 18th CENTURY
NORTH WIRRAL NAMES STILL SURVIVING

Bushel	Oxton
Davenport	Parr
Dawson	Partington
Delamore	Peacock
Dodd	Peers
Godwin	Pemberton
Gould	Powell
Gouldson	Rathbone
Hancock	Rimmer
Ireland	Rowlands
Jackson	Rutter
Jebb	Sherlock
Kemp	Spark
Kendrick	Stanley
Leene	Sutton
Little	Tottey
Lyons	Watmough
Maddock	Wharton
Meadows	Youd

SOME LOCAL PUBS
OF YESTERYEAR
(No longer exist)

Mill Inn	Thingwall
Ring O' Bells	Woodchurch
Horse and Jockey	Woodchurch
Prince of Wales	Irby
Glegg Arms	Thurstaston
Red Cat	Brimstage
Three Pigeons	Heswall
White Lion	Heswall
Ship Inn	Heswall
Farmers Arms	Leighton
Travellers Rest	Upton
New Inn	Greasby

A PAGE FROM WOODCHURCH CHURCH
BAPTISMS AND MARRIAGES 1725-6

Dorothy & William Daughter & Son of William Griffiths of Irby Mariner by Mary his Wife Baptized October 26.

George Son of John Hockenhull of Prenton Esq. Baptized at Bebington Church by Edward Forshall Curate 30 Sept. 1725.

John illegitimate Son of Dorothy Dod by John Nichols Servt. Bapt. Nov 14 1725.

Mary Daughter of Richd. Shaw of Barnston Yeoman by Hanah his Wife Nov. 21 1725.

Lydia Daughter of Peter Parr of Irby Mariner by Catherine his Wife Bap. Dec. 9.

Hugh Son of James Wade of Thingwell Yeoman by Ann his Wife Bap. Jan. 4.

Ellen Daughter of John Hand of Barnston Mariner by Ellen his Wife Bapt. February 15 1725-6

Ellen Daughter of Thomas Pears of Pensby Yeoman by Ellen his Wife Bapt. March 13.

BAPTIZED ANO DONI 1726

Ann Daughter of John Whaley of Pensby Yeoman by Eliz. his Wife Bap. March 29.

William Son of Henry Lea Junior of Barnston by Martha his Wife Baptized April 24.

Thomas Son of Thomas Spark Junior of Oxon Yeoman by Frances his Wife April 28.

Thomas illegitimate son of Ellen Worrall by Tho. Bennett deceased Baptized May 16.

Sarah the Daughter of Joshua Hayes of Barnston Labourer by Mary his Wife June 5.

John Son of Richd. Jackson of Barnston Husbandman by Eliz. his Wife June 26.

Martha Daughter of Hugh Coventry of Woodchurch Cooper by Ellen his Wife Baptized July 31.

Margaret Daughter of Henry Lynaker of Upton Yeoman by Margaret his Wife Bap. August 21.

Ann Daughter of William Gibson of Arrow Yeoman by Mary his Wife Bapt. August 22.

Mary Daughter of John Wharton of Oxon Yeoman by Martha his Wife Bap. August 28.

Peter Son of George Grifiths of Barnston Yeoman by Mary his Wife Baptized Oct. 28.

Esther Daughter of Nathaniel Dawson of Irby Yeoman by Esther his Wife Bap. Nov.1.

Thomas Son of Thomas Gill of Irby Yeoman by Eliz. his Wife Baptized Nov.8.

John Son of Thomas Gregory of Irby Labourer by Katherine his Wife Baptized Nov. 23.

Mary Daughter of John Knowles of Woodchurch Labourer by Mary his Wife Bapt. Nov. 30.

Ann Daughter of Robert Dod of Prenton Taylor by Abigail his Wife Bap. Dec. 4

Alice Daughter of John Reynald of Prenton Joyner by Mary his Wife Baptized December 29 1776

MARRIAGES 1725

Thomas Spark of Oxon Yeoman & Francis Freeman Spinster of Thornton in the Parish of Neston were married May 9 1725 by Richd. Smith Curate by virtue of a licence Pet. Gastrell Chancellor.

Joshua Hayes & Mary Rymmer alias Davies of Pensby in the Parish of Woodchurch Servants were married June 24 1725 Ban. pub. by Richd. Smith Curate.

Matthew Powel Labourer & Mary Potter Spinster both in the Parish were married at Woodchurch August 23 1725. Ban. pub. by Richd. Smith Curate.

BIDSTON CHURCH BAPTISMS 1749

Mary Daugh. of Thos. Hancock Baptiz'd 4th. of May.

Samuel illegitimate Son of Wm. Tenson of Saughan Baptiz'd ye 14th. of May.

Ann ye Daugh. Mat. Powel of Claughton Heath Side Baptiz'd 14th of May.

John Son of John Lea of Moreton Baptiz'd 14th. of May.

William Son of Daniel Smith of Carr Baptiz'd 16th. of May.

Margret Daugh. of Robt. & Eliz. Beyer of Claughton Heath Side Baptiz'd 19th. of May.

Thomas Son of Tho. Evans of Saughan Baptiz'd ye 10th. of July.

William ye Son of William Peers of Claughton Heath Side Baptiz'd the 30th. of July.

Nathaniel Son of John & Elizth. Dawson of Moreton born Octr. ye 20th. Baptiz'd Novr. 21st.

John Son of Wm. & Gwen Hughes of Bidstone Moss Baptiz'd Novr. 19th.

Henry Son of Thos. & Elizth. Appleton Baptized the 30th. of December 1749.

WILL OF PETER DAWSON OF IRBY
BORN 1614 DIED 1672.

In the name of God Amen. March the 26th Anno Dom 1672;
I Petter Dawson of Erbie in the County of Chester Husbandman being sick and weake of body body but of
perfect memory and remembrance praised be God do make and ordaine this my last will and testement in
manner and form following bequest   FFirst I bequeath my soul unto the hands of Almighty God my maker
having through meritorius death and passion Jesus this my Saviour and Redeemer to recieve from pardon
and forgiveness of all my sinnes and as for my body to be buried in the christian buriall at the discretion
of my executors here after nominated I doe give and assign over the house and ground there unto belonging
to my sonne Petter Dawson In I doe give and bequeath all my goods and chattel to pay all my debts and the
over plus if there be any to be equally devided amongst my children ; Charles Coventry owes me eight
shillings and Samuell Fletcher Mason oweth me eleven shillings. Likewise I doe make and ordain Petter
Dawson and Robert Dawson my sonnes to be sole Executors of this my last will and testament revoking all
other wills and testaments as wittenesseth my hand and seale the day and the year first about writton.

Wittnesses
Petter Dawson
William Smith
his – mark
his — mark

Thomas Gouldson

3 Decembris 1672

Coranner J Wainwright

WILL OF NATHANIEL DAWSON YEOMAN
OF TRANMERE BORN 1678 DIED 1753.

Whereas I Nathaniel Dawson of Tranmore in the County of Chester Yeoman being weak of body but of sound and disposing mind and memory do make this my last will and testament in manner and form following.

That is to say first my mind and will is that all my debts funeral expences and probate of this my will be first paid and discharged out of my personel estate.

And I also give and bequeath to my loving wife Esther Dawson all that my messuage tenaments and lands thereunto belonging situate lying and being in Irbie in the said County of Chester with the appurtenanies for and during her natural life if she shall keep herself unmarried and in my name but if she marries again that then and in such case I only give her the third of the said messuage or tenement and lands in Irbie aforesaid for life.

And also I give to my wife Esther a bed bedstock units furniture and a cow at her choice in full of her dower and all her right and title of dower and after her decease or marriage again which of them shall first happen I give and bequeath all the said messuage or tenement and land with this and every of their appurtenanies in Irbie aforesaid to my eldest son John Dawson all his heirs and assigns for ever subject alyable to the payment of the sum of one hundred pounds to and amongst his sisters Ellen Kendrick Catharine Chatterton Ann Newport Ester Dawson and brother Thomas Dawson share and share alike.

And to that end and intent I give and bequeath the said messuage or tenaments and lands in Irbie aforesaid to the Reverend John Crookhall of Woodchurch and William Webster of Greasbie to hold them the said John Crookhall and William Webster their executors administrators and assigns from the day next after the decease or marriage of my said wife Esther (which shall first happen) for and during and unto the full end and term of twenty one years from then to next ensuing and fully to be complete and ended in trust only to raise and recieve out of the rent and proffits of the said messuage or tenaments and lands the said sum of one hundred pounds for the use of my said son Thomas and my daughters Ellen Catharine Ann and Esther aforesaid.

And after the raising and payment those then to and for the use of my son John Dawson his heirs and assigns for the remainder of the said term of twenty one years.

And I also give and bequeath to my son William all my household goods horses cows swines and all my implyments of husbandry whatsoever and also all my living creatures in and about the house and also my farm and estates in Tranmore tenament he selling the proffits of the said tenament this year and paying Mr. Markland my landlord the rent.

If the proffits shall be sufficient to pay the land and what the proffits fall short to pay my mind is that my personal estate shall make out and if it happen that my sons legacy of said goods and cattle after the payment of all rent doth not amount to one hundred pounds then my mind and will is that the rest of my personel estate shall make it up one hundred pounds.

And all the rest of my personal estate not before disposed of I give and bequeath to my said son Thomas Dawson Ellen Kendrick Catharine Chatterton Ann Newport and Esther Dawson in manner following.

That is to say to be divided into five parts one fifth part I give to my son Thomas Dawson another fifth part I give to my daughter Esther Dawson another fifth part I give to my daughter Ann Newport the interest of it only for her life to be by my executors hereafter named but out at interest and after the decease of my said daughter Ann Newport my mind and will is that I do hereby give and bequeath my said daughter Ann Newports share or fifth part of my said personel estate to and amongst all her children as she shall have living at her decease equally amongst them share and share alike.

And I give and bequeath to my daughter Ellen Kendrick another fifth part of my said personal estate within the sum of thirty pounds she having recieved of me several times before that sum or more and I give the said sum of thirty pounds that shall be taken out of my said daughter Ellen Kendricks part to and amongst my said son Thomas Dawson Esther Dawson Catharine Chatterton and Ann Newports children that she shall live at her death she having only the interest for her life.

And I give and bequeath the othe fifth part of my said share of my said personal estate to my daughter Catharine Chatterton.

And I do hereby nominate my loving wife Esther Dawson my son John Dawson and my son William Dawson executive and executors of this my last Will and Testament. In witness whereof I have hereunto set and put my hand and seal this twenty ninth day of January in the year of Our Lord One Thousand Seven Hundred and Fifty Two.

Nathaniel Dawson.

Signed sealed published and declared
by the said testator as and for the
Will and Testament in the presance of
us and by us attested in the presence
of the said testator and the name Catharine
Chatterton being first interlined.
Thomas Lake
John Glegg.

AN INVENTORY OF CATTLE & GOODS & MONEY
OF NATHANIEL DAWSON LATE OF TRANMORE
IN THE COUNTY OF CHESTER. DECEASED.

	£	s	d
To seven cows at 3£ a cow, seven cows more at 4£ a cow	49	0	0
To one cow more, dead at		6	0
To a bull at 2£ 10s two year hieffers at 1£ a heiffer	4	10	0
To two mares one at Six£ the other at 4£	10	0	0
To two geldings one at 5£ 10s the other at 4£ 10s		10	0
Geering for four mares or geldings	1	10	0
To two saddles one at 18s the other at 3s two bridles + a whip 3s	1	4	0
A long cart + wheels at 6£ a muck cart + wheels at 2£	8	0	0
Two plows at 8s two harrows at 10s one large Do. at 7s	1	5	0
A pair of drafts at 5s at set of fellies at 8s a pair of naves at 5s		18	0
A parcel of plow timber at		10	0
One swine a feeding at 1£ 5s one sow at 1£ three pigs at 15s	3	0	0
A furnis pan at 7s a cheese press at 5s a cheese tub at 5s		17	0
Three small tubs at 5s cheespots at 5s two turnils at 2s a churn at 3s		15	0
Pales and milking cans + wooden vesels 6s two half barrels at 5s		11	0
Two beds at 1£ 4s bedstids hangings and there to belonging + a squob at 5s	1	9	0
A clock at 10s a dreser at 10s two corner cubarts at 10s a warming pan 10s	2	0	0
A looking glass at 3s four tables at 16s chairs at 10s two chests at 3s	1	12	0
A large box at 1s a map at 2s a dosen of knives and forks at 3s		6	0
Pewter dishes & plates spoons etc: & potts pans at 1£ 2s a gun 5s	1	7	0
Two pair of settles at 2s a long wheel at 3s two sitting wheels at 5s		10	0
A great & tongs at 8s candlesticks and lanthorns at 2s		10	0
A smoothing iron etc. at 3s stilyards at 3s together with all the irons and brasses in the Nooke at 7s		13	0
A pot cettle + seasepan at 4s mugs and glass bottles at 5s		9	0
Sacks + half measure at 12s sives and ridles at 5s		17	0
a pitch + pilion at 2s aparte of a hide at 6s shovles hooks & mittans1		4	0
A maid & yarn together with all the implyments of husbandry whatsoever that's in + about the house at		10	0
Hay at 2£ 10s straw at 1£ muck at 15s	4	5	0
His boots wairing aparel and cane at	1	10	0
	111	8	0
To about twelve acres of wheat growing on the ground at seven pounds and acre	84	0	0
To cheese and wheat sold	12	0	0
To sixty measures of wheat at 4s 8d a measure	14	0	0
To fourty measures of barley at 2s 6d a measure	5	0	0
To eighty measures of oates at 1s 3d a measure	5	0	0
To four measures paies at 2s 6d a measure		10	0
To a quantity of potatos at		6	0
To money in the House at my Fathers death	65	4	3

5th March 1753 by Wm. Dawson

WILL OF JOHN DAWSON YEOMAN OF MORETON
BORN 1712 DIED 1779

In the name of God Amen. Where as I John Dawson of Moreton in the County of Chester Yeoman knowing the uncertainty of human life do make and ordain this my last will and testament in manner following. That is to say first and principally I recommend my soul into the hands of Almighty God who gave it in hopes to have full and free pardon and forgiveness of all my sins and to inherit everlasting life. And my body I commit to the earth to be orderly and decently buryed.

And as to the disposal of my Estates money goods and chattels as it hath pleased Almighty God to endowe me with I give and bequeath the same as follows. That is to say my mind and will is that all my debts and funeral expences are first paid and discharged by my executrs.

Then I give and bequeath to my loving wife Elizabeth Dawson twenty pounds a year that is twenty pounds of lawfull Brittish money to be paid her every year during her natural life from my Estates in Morton and Upton and likewise the palar and all the goods and furniture that there is in the said palar during her natural life with out paying aneything for the said palar or goods.

Then I give and bequeath to my daughter Margaret Dawson the sum of twelve pounds a year to be paid her every year during her natural life but if she my daughter Margaret Dawson should marry and have any true begotten childeren then after her decease my mind and will is that her childeren that are true begotten chillderen shall and must have the full and just sum of three hundered pounds of lawfull Brittish money to be paid amongst them each an equail share that is to say share and share alike and to be paid them when they arive at the age of twenty one years old.

And my mind and will is that if my daughter Margaret Dawson should die and have no true begoten childeren the three hundered pounds that is herein mentioned for her childeren to have shall and must be equailly divided amongst all my sons and daughters each an equail share that is to say share and share alike.

Then I give and bequeath to my daughter Ann Dawson the sum of three hundered pounds of lawfull Brittish money to be paid her in twelve months after my deceace I also give to my daughter Ester Beard the sum of two hundered and fifty pounds of lawfull Brittish money to be paid her in twelve months after my deceace.

And I also give to my son Nathaniel Dawson the sum of five shillings as I had given him my Estate in Irby before.

Then I give and bequeath to my two sons Peter Dawson and John Dawson all my houses and buildings and all my parceles of land and tenement with all rights titles and prevelages there unto belonging like wise I give to my two sons Peter Dawson and John Dawson all my money and all my stock of cattle and all my implements of husbandary and all my household goods and furniture of what kind or sort soever to occupy use posses and enjoy for there one sole use and benefit against all or any person or persons as shall or cleam aney right or title thereto they my two sons Peter Dawson and John Dawson paying all my lawfull debts and funerall expenses and also all the legusies and money that is herein mentioned to be paid and for them to pay each an equal share of the legucies that are herein mentioned and likewise they my two sons Peter Dawson and John Dawson are and must have each an equal share of my Estates and all my money and personally here before mentioned to be equailly divided betwixt them share and share alike.

And I do nominate and appoint my loving wife Elizabeth Dawson and my son Peter Dawson Executors of this my last will and testemen and hereby revoke disanul and make voide all former wills by me before made, and do gratifie and confirm this and no other to be my only true last will and testement

In witness here of I John Dawson interchangably have here unto set and put my hand and seal this eighth day of May in the nintenth year of the Reign of our Soverigne Lord George the third King of Great Britain & in the year of our Lord one thousand seven hundered and seventy nine signed sealed declared and published in the prisence,

> *Saml. Wathen*

of us

> *George Meadow*
> *Thomas Meadow*
> > *Jn. Dawson*
> > *12th July 1779*

Peter Dawson the Extor. in this Will named took the usual oath of an Extor. in comon form Power being reserved to Elizth. Dawson Widow the extor. of

and 300£   before
> *J Briggs*

Probate issued
July 12th sametime

PRINTED WITH KIND PERMISSION OF CHESHIRE COUNTY COUNCIL ARCHIVES AND LOCAL STUDIES. WS 1783

SKETCH OF THINGWALL IN 1850 WITH FIELD NAMES

FIELDS HAVE RINGED NUMBERS TO INDICATE WHICH PROPERTIES THEY BELONGED TO. EG. (17) BELONGS TO "THINGWALL FARM." 17

1. THINGWALL HALL, YARD AND LODGE. OWNER J. LILLEY.
2. COTTAGE. OWNER AND OCCUPIER T. WILLIAMS.
3. MILL FARM. OWNER. R. VYNER OCCUPIER T. LYON
4. POPLAR COTTAGE. OWNER R. VYNER OCCUPIER T. JOHNSON
5. COTTAGE. OWNER J. ROBERTS OCCUPIER G. WILLIAMS
6. THINGWALL HOUSE. OWNER AND OCCUPIER MISS E. WADE
7. MILL HOUSE. OWNER AND OCCUPIER S. CAPPER.
8. MILL YARD.
9. MILLERS COTTAGE. OWNER S. CAPPER. OCCUPIER. T. MEDCALF
10. HEATHFIELD COTTAGE. OWNER J. BELLYSE. TENNANT. S. CAPPER.
11. THE FIDDLERS FOLLEY. OWNER R. VYNER. OCCUPIER T. GERRARD.
12. COMMON FARM OWNER R. VYNER OCCUPIER H. KEMP
13. BARN FARM — OWNER J. SHAW OCCUPIER T. JACKSON
14. MANOR FARM OWNER J. ROBERTS OCCUPIER W. WHITBY

15. WOODFINLOW FARM. OWNER J. BELLYSE. TENNANT J. REES
16. LODGE FARM OWNER J. LEECH. OCCUPIER J. JAFFS
17. THINGWALL FARM OWNER R. VYNER OCCUPIER R. ROBINSON

A. TOPHOUSE FARM IN ARROWE TOWSHIP OWNER R. SHAW. OCCUPIER MARY KENDRICK RENTED SOME FIELDS IN THINGWALL MARKED (A) OWNED BY LORD R. VYNER.

· COMMONS AND QUARRIES. OWNERS PROPRIETORS OF THE TOWNSHIP OF THINGWALL, THEMSELVES

PRENTON BROOK

LANDICAN TOWNSHIP
STORETON TOWNSHIP
BARNSTON TOWNSHIP
PENSBY TOWNSHIP
IRBY TOWNSHIP
ARROW TOWNSHIP
BARNSTON TOWNSHIP

LANDICAN BROOK
DALE END BROOK

TO IRBY
TO BARNSTON
TO PENSBY

DALE HEAD
LOWER HAY
BREACH HAY
DALE HAY
DALE HAY
LITTLE HAY
WHELPERS
WHELPERS
NEW MEADOW
BREACH HAY
DALE SHOOT
GREEN HAY
SHOCKING DALE
GORSEY HILL
SWANS
SWANS
BACKSIDE MEADOW
LITTLE MEADOW
CART GAP
HAY FIELD
THINGWELL COMMON
CROFT
MARLED HAY
GALA PITS
MEADOW
RYE HAY
CORN HILL
CROSS HILL
CROSS HILL
MARL HAY
MILL HAY
CROSS HILL GATE
TOP OUT GATES
CROSS HAY
CROSS HILL
MARLED HAY
MILL FIELD
HIGHER HAY
DITCH
TOP OUT GATES
TOP OUT GATES
FOLLY
MILL HAY
MILL FIELD
MILL FIELD
BLEAK LOOMS
STONEY WALL
TWO LOAVES
WARRENS
MILL HAY
CROFT
SANDY HAY
SAND HAY
NEW HAY
MONEY PITS
TWO LOAVES
BIG TWO LOAVES
NEW FIELD
PART OF NEW HAY
OLD HEATH FIELD
HEATH FIELD
TWO LOAVES
HEATH FIELD
LITTLE TWO LOVES
NEW HEATH FIELD
NEW HEATH FIELD
NEAR HEATH FIELD
HEATH FIELD
HEATH FIELD
THE MISTAKE
MIDDLE HEATH FIELD
FAR HEATH FIELD
TOP HOUSE FARM
PITS
CROFT
CROFT
BENTY HEATH FARM (IN IRBY)

Thingwall 1850

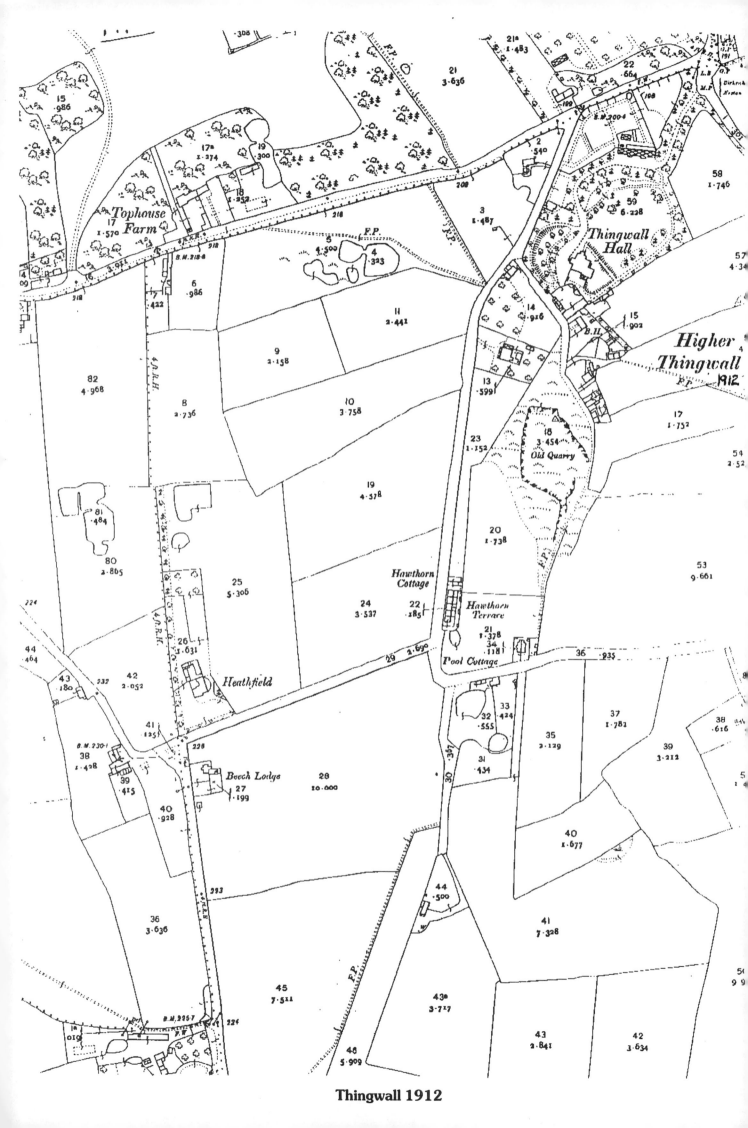

Thingwall 1912

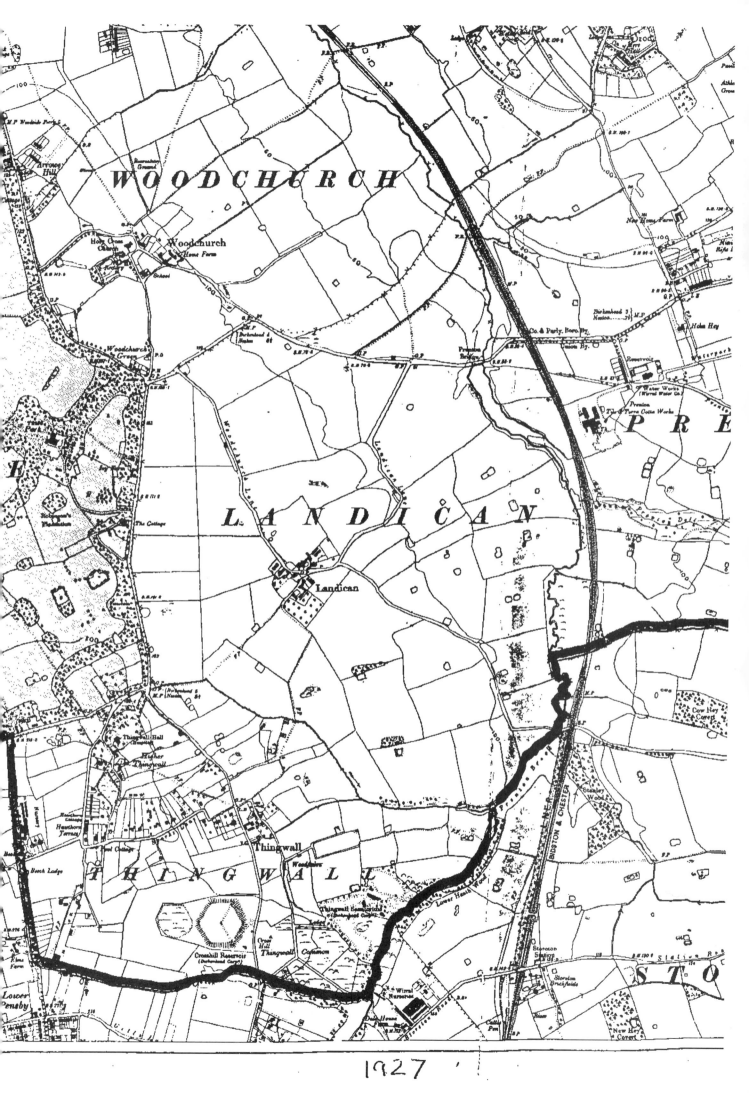

1927

Landican 1927

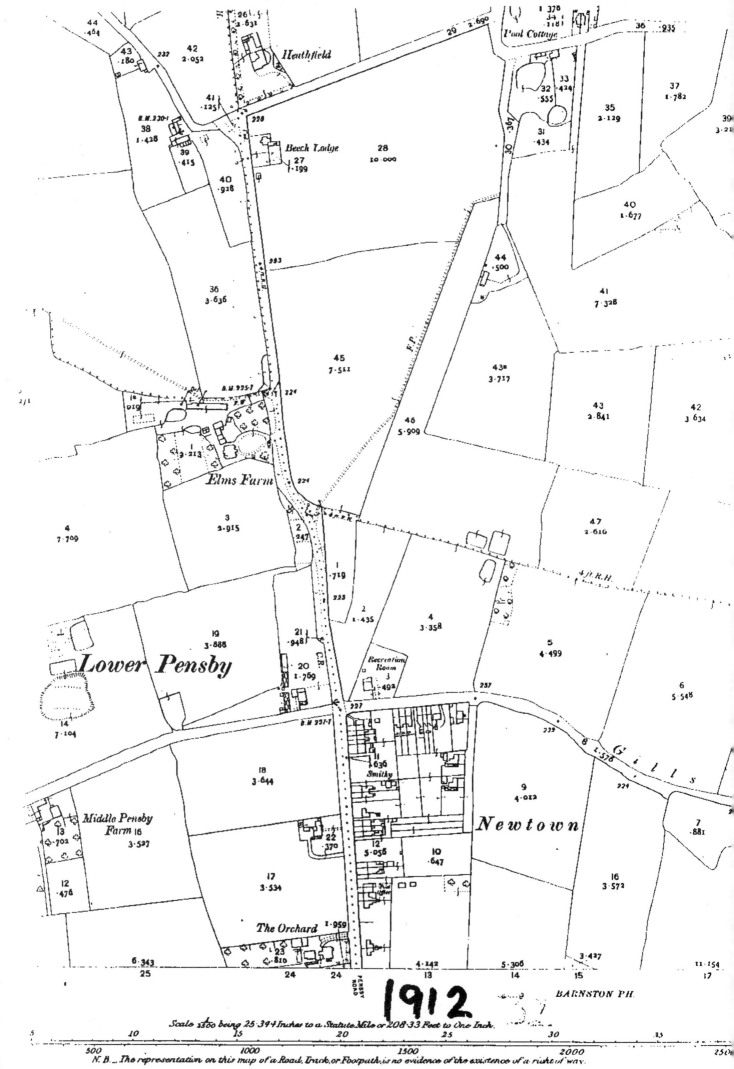

Scale 1:2500 being 25·344 Inches to a Statute Mile or 208·33 Feet to One Inch.

N. B.— The representation on this map of a Road, Track, or Footpath is no evidence of the existence of a right of way.

Lower Pensby 1912